WENSLEY CLARKSON
BORN TO KILL

D1637732

WENSLEY CLARKSON

BORN TO KILL

**THE TWISTED LIFE AND BIZARRE DEATH OF THE
MAN WHO MURDERED GIANNI VERSACE**

JOHN BLAKE

For Polly and Rosie

Published by John Blake Publishing Ltd,
3, Bramber Court, 2 Bramber Road,
London W14 9PB, England

www.blake.co.uk

First published in paperback in 2004

ISBN 1 84454 038 3

British Library Cataloguing-in-Publication Data:

A catalogue record for this book is available from the British Library.

Design by www.envydesign.co.uk

Printed in Great Britain by Bookmarque

1 3 5 7 9 10 8 6 4 2

Text copyright Wensley Clarkson, 2004

Papers used by John Blake Publishing are natural, recyclable products made
from wood grown in sustainable forests. The manufacturing processes conform to
the environmental regulations of the country of origin.

Every attempt has been made to contact the relevant copyright-holders, but
some were unobtainable. We would be grateful if the appropriate people
could contact us.

NOTES OF GRATITUDE

The idea of using a leaden, dispassionate word like "acknowledgments" for this section cannot begin to express the depth of my feelings for the many individuals who have made this book possible. I owe them my deepest and most heartfelt gratitude.

First to my literary manager Peter Miller and my editor Charles Spicer. Without them this book would never have happened. Their support and guidance have been very much appreciated. Also, many, many thanks to Uri, David, and Michelle and the rest of the team at PMA. Also, Peter Wilson, who first brought this case to my attention and whose investigative skills have proved so invaluable in helping me put this book together.

In San Diego and San Francisco numerous friends and associates of Andrew Cunanan helped enormously despite fears for their own safety. Many of them asked that their names be kept confidential. I have respected their wishes and therefore cannot thank them by name.

Then there is my worldwide network of Brendan Bourne, Anthony Bowman and Mark Sandelson in California, John Glatt in New York, Jack Green in Minneapolis, Tony Benwell in Chicago. Also the FBI and police departments of all the cities mentioned in this book. And John Taylor in London.

But one of my biggest debts of gratitude goes to the many friends and colleagues who kept me constantly updated so as to make this book the most up-to-the-minute version of events.

Après moi, le déluge—"After me, disaster"

—The caption Andrew Cunanan chose for his high school yearbook.

AUTHOR'S NOTE

Andrew Cunanan, the man whose life is described in this book, fits the commonly used definition of a spree killer because he was engaged full-time in the business of killing one person after another.

"Spree killers are a type of serial killer who are involved on a full-time basis in their killings and in running from the law," says James Alan Fox, dean of the college of criminal justice at Northeastern University.

Ordinary serial killers, by contrast, says Professor Fox, may have jobs and families and take time out between their murders.

Some experts believe that a spree or serial killer must claim three victims before being given the appellation, but Professor Fox believes that four is a more accurate figure.

Cunanan was forever inventing fictional personas for himself. I have pieced together the story of his life in part from what he told friends about himself and his family. But how much was reality and how much was his invention is, of course, difficult to know. But fact or fantasy, it all is essential to understanding who Cunanan was.

DEATH AT EVERY STOP

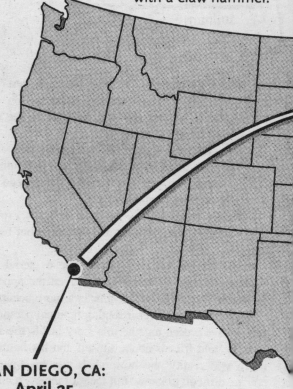

MINNEAPOLIS, MN: April 29
Jeffrey Trail is found beaten to death
with a claw hammer.

**SAN DIEGO, CA:
April 25**

Andrew Cunanan
leaves for Minnesota.

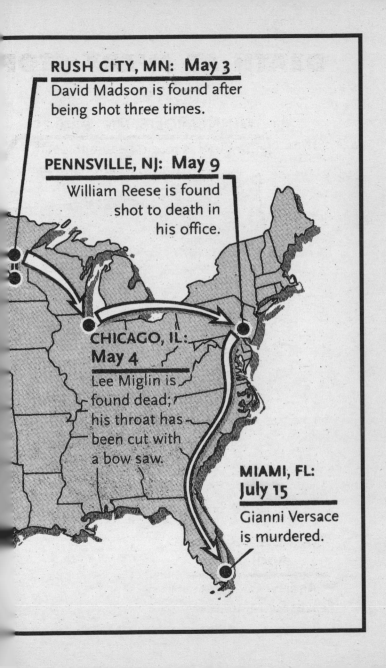

RUSH CITY, MN: May 3
David Madson is found after being shot three times.

PENNSVILLE, NJ: May 9
William Reese is found shot to death in his office.

CHICAGO, IL: May 4
Lee Miglin is found dead; his throat has been cut with a bow saw.

MIAMI, FL: July 15
Gianni Versace is murdered.

Prologue

Sliding across the rainbow from erotic pink to lizard green, the Art Deco structures on Ocean Drive, Miami Beach, were built to uplift the spirits of Americans and offer a distraction from the Great Depression.

Over sixty years later, they had helped turn the beach area into a gaudy, head-turning district filled with eye-candy buildings. Tacky, faddish, and full of showgirl simplicity. They also helped Ocean earn the local nickname of "Deco Drive."

Only fifteen years earlier, this area was better known for its derelict buildings, prostitutes, and cocaine dealers. Today, it's South Beach, the deco darling of the world and a mecca for the area's vast gay population.

Throngs of bronzed and beautiful people filled the district. They rollerbladed and strolled past the tables of places like the popular News Cafe, on Ocean Drive, along the sidewalks through the early morning traffic, beneath the palm trees, the wedding-cake deco hotels, and a sparkling golden Miami sun.

The News Cafe, favorite haunt of the fashionable and beautiful, is on the beachside boulevard that Miami's rich and successful residents helped turn from a rundown, sleazy oceanfront into an American Riviera.

Ten years ago, this was Skid-Row-sur-Mer, and the main businesses were single shots of cocaine and hard liquor. Now it is transformed. Grunge never made it here, nor did the fear of skin cancer; there is little suntan lotion below the factor six on sale.

The arrival of celebrities like Madonna, Sylvester Stallone, and a galaxy of others confirmed the revival of Miami Beach to its glory days of the Roaring Twenties, when the police department had to put up boards on the sand to remind the bathing belles: "Warning: Law Requires Full Bathing Suit."

The manager of the News Cafe, Ron McLean, even notched himself a place in city history. He set up the News Cafe in 1989, a twenty-four-hour restaurant and bar, another symbol of Miami Beach's renaissance.

The idea of selling foreign newspapers as well as eggs Benedict and margaritas turned out to have been inspired. It became a mecca for many of the area's most beautiful people.

The News Cafe also happened to be a regular start-of-the-day haunt for a gray-haired, balding middle-aged figure in white T-shirt, black shorts and sandals. Although on the morning of Tuesday, July 15, 1997, he seemed more agitated than usual.

Cafe hostess Stephanie Vanover, thirty, even noticed that on that day he approached the restaurant from the opposite, beach side, of the street, which was unusual. She had actually seen him walk right past the premises before crossing the street and returning "in a sort of loop."

When he greeted Stephanie he was definitely less relaxed than usual. At the counter of the restaurant's newstand, the man spent $15.01 on five magazines: *Business Week, Vogue, Entertainment Weekly, People,* and *The New Yorker.* He asked for *Time* magazine as well, but the store did not have it in stock.

4

Then the man departed, strolled past a group of tourists staking out places on the beach, and walked the four blocks to his home at 1116 Ocean Drive.

Shortly before nine A.M., as he pulled out his keys to unlock the black wrought-iron gates to his palatial, multimillion-dollar home, another younger man in his mid-twenties suddenly approached. He was dressed in gray muscle T-shirt, black shorts, black baseball cap, and tennis shoes. There was an exchange of words. Witnesses later claimed that both men were cursing each other in Italian.

The younger man then took a heavy .40 caliber pistol out from his backpack and shot his victim in the head. The man fell as the first bullet hit him. Then the gunman coolly and calmly bent down to put a second bullet into his skull.

The magazines spilled from his arms onto the steps. They were soon stained in his blood.

Meanwhile the gunman pocketed his gun and walked into a crowd of nearby shoppers, leaving his victim dying on the coral-pink steps to the mansion.

Eddie Bianchi was at a nearby rollerblade store when he heard the two shots. Bianchi rushed out of the store and saw the middle-aged man lying on the steps of a nearby house. He was face-up and shaking. There was a man walking in and out of the house in a daze. There was also a woman screaming, "I saw him! I saw him!"

"We were right there watching and there's nothing you can do," Bianchi recalled shortly afterwards. "His blood was coming out like crazy. He shook a little bit and stopped moving."

Police and paramedics arrived at the scene within minutes, but it was already too late.

Detectives quickly recovered two cartridge cases from the steps. Then one of the officers spotted a dead pigeon lying at the bottom of the steps, just a few feet from the body. Was it a symbol left by the killer or just a coincidence?

*   *   *

Finally, among those magazines scattered on the steps to the mansion was People. *It had just carried a profile of a serial killer who had recently been added to the FBI's Ten Most Wanted List: his name was Andrew Phillip Cunanan and that morning he had just claimed his fifth victim.*

One

BORN TO DIE

Almost twenty-eight years earlier, Andrew Phillip Cunanan was born in San Diego, California, on August 31, 1969.

Without smog, junglelike entwinements of freeways, or shocking extremes of wealth and poverty, San Diego is supposed to represent the acceptable face of Southern California, with many of the region's appealing features but few of its bad habits.

Eclipsed by Los Angeles in the race to become *the* Southern Californian city, San Diego was for a long time thought of as an insignificant location between LA and Mexico. But by the time Andrew Cunanan was born at the end of the so-called Swinging Sixties, it had assumed a comfortable mantle all of its own.

Built on a gracefully curving bay, San Diego was not only scenically inviting, it also possessed a range of museums among America's finest, plus an evocative and nowadays well-tended history.

Basking in almost constant sunshine and with its humidity tempered by its close proximity to the Pacific Ocean, the national image of San Diego as healthy, affluent, and conservative was very true to a large extent.

And for the first few years of his life, Andrew Cunanan

probably could not have wished for a better place to be brought up.

He wanted for nothing. Cunanan's Philippine-born father Modesto was a former U.S. naval officer who'd turned to stockbroking. His thirty-year-old mother MaryAnn was a deeply religious Catholic who took young Andrew to mass very regularly from an early age.

Modesto D. Cunanan, thirty-five, and MaryAnn had married on May 25, 1961. Mr. Cunanan was serving in the U.S. Navy and stationed in San Diego at the time.

After his retirement in 1972, the family moved to Rancho Bernardo, a middle-class community in the hills overlooking the city. Andrew Cunanan was the youngest of four children and was to remain the baby of his family for his entire childhood.

By the age of six he could read the Bible from cover to cover. At the age of ten he regularly read an encyclopedia at bedtime. And at school he was soon proclaimed to have an above-average IQ.

The only disturbing sound that became a familiar feature of Cunanan's early childhood was that of the constant stream of the freight trains blowing their horns at all times of the day and night as they shunted across the dozens of level crossings spread through the San Diego below.

But as Cunanan turned into a talkative, highly intelligent—and somewhat spoiled—child, so his father became increasingly withdrawn as his stockbroking work became more and more pressurized. Perhaps afraid to admit to his young family that his job was not working out so well, he began coming home late.

When Cunanan was still in elementary school, he later insisted to many of his friends, his father disciplined him very hard, claiming to have suffered bruises on his back and stomach. Modesto Cunanan took the attitude that children need strong parental discipline.

By the time Andrew Cunanan reached twelve, he was a strikingly handsome dark-haired boy, five-foot-eight in height with a well-defined face with strong eyebrows, and deep, dark, slightly slanted saucerlike brown eyes.

Cunanan's parents decided that in order to take full advantage of their son's obvious intelligence they would financially stretch themselves and send him to a highly reputable private school called Bishop's, in San Diego.

Within months of arriving at the exclusive school—fees $7,000 a year—Cunanan began to realize that he could get just about anything he wanted by using an irresistible combination of good looks and charm.

Cunanan also possessed a determined streak that made him seem much brighter than many of his classmates. He also had a biting wit and a photographic memory that astonished many of his friends and teachers.

"He never forgot anyone's names and he recognized people's faces before they even had a chance to introduce themselves," said one childhood friend, Scott Wagner.

Ultimately, Cunanan was the overpampered child of a mother who he would describe as overbearing and overloving, who had made it clear to him from a very early age that he should make a real success of his life.

Cunanan attributed to his mother's influence his ability to use his charm and good looks. But he felt confused about his emotions toward the boys and girls in his class. Some of those girls scared him more than the boys because they were so pushy about wanting him to date them, even at that early age.

He kept comparing them to his adoring mom and none of them matched up to her. Some of the boys in his class were jealous of his good looks and Cunanan often found himself being bullied in the school yard between classes. He felt more attracted to the weaker, quieter children—and many of them were male.

Back at home, Cunanan was always good about helping his mom out in the house. Some of the Cunanan's relatives were amazed at how well house-trained the youngster was. He seemed to be forever clearing up after folks. It bothered some of them because schoolboys were not usually so neat and tidy.

Cunanan enjoyed keeping the house spic-and-span. He wanted to ensure it was a home to be proud of when he invited a friend back from school. But Cunanan soon discovered that his domineering mother's embarrassing questions meant he was better off hanging out at friends' houses instead. MaryAnn, it seemed to Cunanan, was a very possessive mother who insisted on vetting all her son's friends to see if they were suitable.

But that didn't stop Cunanan from always remembering to give his mother birthday cards and gifts and Mother's Day cards. Their closeness was noticeable to many of their relatives.

"When Andrew was young he seemed to be virtually attached to his mother. They almost never went anywhere without each other," one relative later explained.

Cunanan also developed what was to become a virtually lifelong obsession with clothes. Even in his early teens, Cunanan would buy an average of one new shirt every week. And he constantly changed the style of his dark, thick hair.

At Bishop's, some of his classmates began to question his sexuality. But they were still all too young to linger on the subject.

Cunanan did not get along well with his father following that first instance of physical discipline on him. But, like many children, he in some ways blamed himself for what had happened. He knew his father was having a tough time at work and he desperately didn't want to cause problems between his parents. In later life, the very thought of what his father had done to him would make him very angry, but

12

as a child he felt a strange sense of guilt, which constantly ate away at him.

Following more examples of his father's "discipline," Cunanan's self-destructive personality began to emerge.

As a child, Cunanan apparently did not receive the sensory stimulation he required from his family and increasingly found it difficult to establish a boundary between himself and the world beyond his adoring mother. He was becoming an all-encompassing individual, seeing things from his own perspective and no one else's.

Other family members soon noticed how fearless Cunanan became and the way he would try to manipulate situations to suit himself and no one else. He also seemed incapable of appreciating it when he hurt other people's feelings. Whenever Cunanan did something bad he seemed to feel little remorse and certainly showed little sympathy for his victim.

But beneath the bubbling, handsome exterior there lay within Cunanan an inner sadness caused primarily by the fact that he found it incredibly difficult to enjoy any childlike preoccupations. Childhood was supposed to be a pleasurable experience in which the developing individual learned how to be happy and derive happiness from as many situations as possible. But Cunanan's brothers and sisters were much older and his few childhood friends soon came to the conclusion that he was not capable of enjoying things in the normal sense of the word.

"Andrew would always be daydreaming. He didn't say much and we all kinda ignored him," one old school friend revealed many years later.

Then there were the dreams that Cunanan said he experienced as a child; the continuum of reality was so often shattered by nightmares that seemed to project such horrific images that he found it impossible to believe that his life could be happy. Weird images of death and destruction filled these dreams, but there was one overriding character who would keep featuring in these nightmares—his father. Strangely, Cunanan found those dreams to be as pleasurable as they were fearful.

But Cunanan's sleeping fantasies had their own twisted symbology, steeped in terror of some dreadful memories and fears that seemed to be permanently stored in his mind. However, according to certain friends and family, the most disturbing aspect of all this for the young Cunanan was that sometimes he said he would find himself in a half-dreaming, half-waking state that combined memories and terrors with the reality of some of his experiences at the hands of his father, or some other demonlike figure.

He found those dreamlike fantasies intruding upon his life with increasing frequency. Without warning he would often find himself in a world of his own terror-filled nightmares with no basis for determining whether he was dreaming or waking.

In these dreams, people's identities and sexuality would become confused. Cunanan, even from a young age, became more and more locked inside that fantasy world while the real world seemed to be filled with people without real identity or meaning.

Like so many before him, Cunanan kept trying to convince himself when he was a child that he would never punish his own children in the way his father had done to him. Increasingly, he began to grow bitter about the whole concept of families because he believed that they were all unhappy like his. He promised himself he would stay unmarried and happy. Andrew Cunanan had no intention of repeating history.

Cunanan was just thirteen years old when he had his first sexual experience with an older youth he met in a San Diego park. Instead of feeling any shame or guilt about the encounter, Cunanan proudly told a few of his classmates about the encounter. He was already openly referring to his own homosexuality.

"Andrew would suddenly come out with the weirdest stories," explained one old school friend. "And he didn't seem inhibited about his sexuality. We were shocked by some of his stories. He seemed to have no shame."

In fact, Cunanan was rather proud of his exploits because, as he told his friends, he'd been thinking constantly about sex since the age of eleven.

A number of casual sexual experiences followed and Cunanan would relish telling some of his classmates what happened, irrelevant of whether or not they wanted to hear.

"He was so proud of sleeping with guys," one old school friend later recalled. "We were all pretty fazed by his attitude towards sex."

At fourteen, Cunanan embarked on a sexual relationship with a much older man he met in San Diego. This time he was much more secretive about the identity of his new lover.

His school friend later recalled: "As usual, Andrew was real proud of his adventures, but he wouldn't tell any of us the name of this guy. We all reckoned he had to be someone well known in the community."

Cunanan eventually admitted to friends that his new, much older, lover was married with children and that was why he kept his identity such a secret. At one stage there were even rumors that Cunanan's lover actually had his children at the same school as Cunanan, but these claims were never substantiated.

However that older lover represented Cunanan's first taste of the good life. His older friend had paid for everything for him from meals in restaurants to a constant flow of gifts including expensive watches and jewelry.

Cunanan was already doggedly determined to live life in the fast lane. Cunanan's other brothers and sisters had long since left the family home and his parents were so preoccupied with their own problems that they never gave his late-night absences any real thought.

Even in his early teens, Andrew Cunanan had already decided that he would do whatever it took to make sure he had everything he wanted and needed without making a commitment to a normal life like the rest of his unhappy family.

One of his first moves in that direction was to start changing his name on a regular basis.

By the age of fifteen, Cunanan was five feet, ten inches tall, fairly muscular and looked at least eighteen. He began frequenting some of the gay bars and clubs in San Diego's primarily homosexual district of Hillcrest.

He didn't particularly like his last name because he felt it made him sound Filipino. He preferred to reinvent himself as a Latino. That seemed much more glamorous and impressive to any would-be suitors. Sometimes he'd become Andrew DeSilva, other times David Morales.

And when he wanted to be posher he'd become Drew or Andrew Philip, the trainee art dealer.

Cunanan liked the freedom that changing his name gave him. It meant he could invent entire life stories about himself, embellishing these accounts with extra detail that were deliberately intended to make him more attractive to potential male partners.

Changing his name also meant he could distance himself from his family and all their problems, not to mention the discipline he had suffered at the hands of his father.

For beneath his lively, charming exterior, a highly complex character was already emerging. There was also an apparent streak of naked ambition to get whatever he wanted by whatever means possible.

His on-off affair with that older married man became even more serious when the man decided to rent an apartment in the Hillcrest district for the couple's love trysts. Cunanan soon began visiting the apartment—he had his own key—with other men when his older lover was not around.

That apartment became the perfect means of escape from all the unhappiness at his family home in nearby Rancho Bernardo. Sometimes, he even went to the apartment alone, just to give himself time to think about his life and loves.

Cunanan didn't particularly like what he'd already become at a very young age, but at least in the apartment he could be himself and take a step back and consider things from a fresh perspective.

But, inevitably, life at that apartment eventually turned sour for Cunanan after he and his lover fell out when the older man discovered an article of clothing left by one of Cunanan's other male lovers.

Soon after that Cunanan was asked to leave permanently. The thought of only being able to go to his unhappy home appalled Cunanan. The atmosphere at the house had become tense every time he made an appearance because his parents had grown increasingly concerned by his lengthy absences.

Cunanan told them it was none of their business. They were worried because it seemed as if their youngest son was slipping away from them right in front of their eyes.

But Cunanan had no real choice but to stay at home. He was only fifteen and there was nowhere else for him to turn. He was after all, still attending school.

In Rancho Bernardo, Cunanan's return to the fold was greeted by smotherings of love and kisses from his mother MaryAnn, who still had no idea that her son was a practicing homosexual. She was just relieved that he didn't seem to be spending so much time away from the house.

Cunanan's father Modesto was not so welcoming. He had his suspicions about his son's sexuality, but was far too remote a personality to talk openly about his thoughts.

In any case, father and son hadn't really communicated properly since Modesto began severely disciplining him years previously. The discipline was a thing of the past, but the memories of them still lingered on.

However, MaryAnn Cunanan was this time determined not to lose her "baby," so she persuaded her increasingly cash-strapped husband to buy his son a birthday gift that would surely guarantee he would remain in the family home.

Two

MOM'S THE WORD

MaryAnn Cunanan was beaming with pleasure as she woke her son Andrew to wish him a happy sixteenth birthday. Cunanan thought she was just being her usual overbearing self until he was urged to look outside the window of their single-story home in Rancho Bernardo.

Cunanan literally couldn't believe his eyes. There, gleaming on the driveway was a used red Nissan 300ZX sports car. It was then that Andrew Cunanan fully realized how determined his domineering mother was to have him back living with the family following his summer escapades.

While his father Modesto said little that morning, it was Cunanan's mother who made all the fuss of her birthday boy. Cunanan knew full well that she must have really twisted his father's arm to get him to pay out $5,000 for the vehicle.

That sports car should have been a happy turning point in Andrew Cunanan's life. It was supposed to represent a gift from a loving family. But he saw it an entirely different way, as he told one school friend.

"It just made me realize how pathetic they all were. They think that after all that's happened they can just buy back my love," Cunanan sneered to his friend.

Back at the exclusive Bishop's School in San Diego, Cunanan proudly showed off his car and joked with his friends that now he could "go prowling for pretty boys to make love to."

By this time Cunanan was studying French and theater at school. He had a good ear for languages and had already mastered Spanish and Italian.

Cunanan also continued to amuse his classmates with his flamboyancy. There certainly never was a dull moment when Andrew Cunanan was around.

One time he surpassed his own highly questionable levels of good taste by attending a school function in a red patent leather jumpsuit.

"Andrew screeched up to the school gates in his Toyota and jumped out dressed in this bizarre outfit which seemed about three sizes too tight," explained one fellow Bishop's student. "Then he proudly announced to us that it had been a gift from a much older man who he'd been dating."

Cunanan was considered highly eccentric but very amusing company by both straight and gay students at Bishop's.

"You'd think he'd get bullied by the macho sports jocks, but everyone was happy to tolerate Andrew because he was a bit like the court jester. He was so unashamedly gay that it prevented anyone from taking offense. What you saw was what you got," explained an old classmate.

In 1987, aged eighteen, Cunanan graduated and perhaps not so surprisingly, his classmates voted him as the student "Least Likely to be Forgotten."

His own yearbook quote was a misrendering of the haughty declaration often attributed to Louis XV: "*Apres moi, le deluge.*" Translated it means, "After me, disaster."

Cunanan then enrolled at the University of California in San Diego majoring in history, although his priorities clearly revolved around his gay lifestyle.

At home, Cunanan's parents were relieved that their youngest son appeared to be getting down to his studies. Cunanan had already told them quite clearly that he had aspirations to be an actor.

But there was another obsession—not so clearcut but just as meaningful in Cunanan's mind. He was driven by an obsession to live whereever and with whom he wanted.

In some of San Diego's gay bars and clubs, Cunanan had already become well known as someone who would frequently come in with older men.

One of his most regular friends was a wealthy older businessman.

The first night Cunanan met the man, they slept together and his friends on the gay circuit teased him that he was becoming "an easy lay." But Cunanan did not look at it like that. He was proud of his conquest of this man and, typically, openly talked about details of their sexual encounter.

But many of Cunanan's friends were surprised that the fit, young handsome teenager should allow himself to get embroiled in a relationship with such an older man.

He was just eighteen. But what they failed to notice was that this older suitor was providing Cunanan with an entrée into the richer social circles of San Diego.

And Cunanan did not consider himself a cheap hustler, not even a high-class prostitute. He was something more subtle and refined: a worthy companion.

Cunanan went to a lot of effort to find out about the sort of things he knew would be discussed at dinner tables. And he was a very fast learner.

"He knew the right kind of fork to use, the right cognac to drink," San Diego social columnist Nicole Ramirez-Murray recalled.

"I remember one time people were talking about what Henry Kissinger was up to, and Cunanan jumped right in. He was in a class of his own as a gigolo."

One target of opportunity was Gamma Mu, an exclusive

fraternity of wealthy, mostly gay men who could bestow nice gifts like the $30,000 car given to him by one older lover.

On the Gamma Mu circuit, Andrew Cunanan had rapidly become a popular date for older gay men. He was clean-cut, handsome, well read, and extremely charming.

Cunanan actually had his mother to thank in many ways for improving himself with such ease. Her nonstop advice about only picking rich and successful friends definitely rubbed off on her son, although she still refused to accept that her beloved "baby" son was gay.

On a more mundane level, Cunanan's overriding problem was that he adored himself physically above anyone else. He was always glancing in the mirror, combing his thick, wavy dark hair and sometimes he'd even dab a little mascara onto his eyelashes to make sure he'd get every man's attention whenever he walked into a bar, club, or cafe.

It was a brilliant routine in many ways and Cunanan found he enjoyed it so much that he was convinced that one day he would make it as a full-time actor. He even started occasionally doing extra work in Los Angeles although it often meant a day trip to LA and back following a rejection at an audition.

Cunanan's elderly benefactor was undoubtedly very kind toward him, but Cunanan was ultimately more interested in a relationship with his own alter ego rather than anyone else.

"Andrew was more in love with himself than anyone else," explained James Coburn, a friend from San Diego. "In a perfect world he would have liked to find a man just like himself but a little older and much richer."

Cunanan's older partner eventually became very irritated because Cunanan did not pay him enough attention. After all, this man was supporting both of them on the San Diego gay social circuit.

* * *

Cunanan's other big problem was that he was promiscuous. It was a subconscious attempt to be loved by everyone. Cunanan had no problem picking up new male companions and seemed unworried by the AIDS epidemic that was sweeping the U.S. at the time.

He even told some friends that his father was gay and Modesto Cunanan would fly in with a lover his son's age, and the three of them would ride around in a Rolls Royce.

It was all sheer fantasy but it helped keep Andrew Cunanan's name on everyone's mind. People were talking about him constantly.

On the studies front, Cunanan was not impressing the staff at the University of Southern California, in San Diego. His coursework was either sloppy or simply never handed in. He was a man with a lot of unsuitable diversions.

"Andrew had become the ultimate gay party animal," old San Diego friend Gary Danes said later. "He'd also found out that it was relatively easy to survive if you hooked up with the right guys in town."

Some days, Cunanan would skip class at college and wander around the construction sites in the center of San Diego admiring handsome, muscular male workers.

One time, he proudly told a friend many years later, he hung around a site for a man he'd earlier spotted and the two of them went to the man's house and had sex. Cunanan didn't even bother to ask his name.

Another time, the inevitable occurred when Cunanan was walking arm in arm smooching with a man along a street in San Diego and his mother and father drove by. He only saw them when it was too late and knew they'd spotted him.

Cunanan was extremely upset that his parents had seen him with a man. He didn't mind the rest of the world being aware of his sexual persuasion, but he didn't want his parents to know.

For many days following that incident, Cunanan couldn't

face talking to his mother or father about what they'd seen. Neither MaryAnn—who was in complete denial about all of her son's habits—or father Modesto really wanted to know the truth despite what they had seen.

Meanwhile back on the San Diego gay circuit, Cunanan was continuing to put up a nonstop facade of the bright and breezy guy who could be anyone's friend. However beneath the surface, darkness was starting to appear on the horizon.

Being the handsome young, tanned, companion to numerous men had been an enjoyable, attention-seeking role since his early teens, but as he got a little older he found that some of the men he slept with had a different agenda from those older, more gentle males he'd originally been with.

On two or three occasions in San Diego, he told one friend many years later, he went back to men's apartments and found himself forced to take part in bondage and sadomasochistic scenes that could have ended in serious injury. Still only a very young man, Cunanan recalled to his friends that the beatings reminded him of what his father had done to him when he was younger. He was upset but, typically, also curious about the motives behind such men's brutal sexuality.

Cunanan's parents still hadn't properly tackled Cunanan's homosexuality, but the teenager got the distinct impression that they had accepted he was gay and there was nothing they could do about it.

Modesto Cunanan's attitude toward his son softened at this time. He was resigned to losing his job as a stockbroker and it later emerged that Mr. Cunanan was even suspected of embezzling tens of thousands of dollars of customers' money.

The prospect of ending his career made Modesto Cunanan far more reasonable to deal with, or so his son found. They even had some reasonably long conversations after meals and

Modesto indicated he was sorry for the discipline he'd inflicted on his son all those years earlier.

Andrew Cunanan was very encouraged by his father's attitude. He seemed far more friendly toward his son. Cunanan even felt a bond emerge between them, but his mother was not impressed.

Cunanan remained her "baby boy," and she didn't like the feeling that her husband and son were ganging up on her. All the other children had long since left home and now she was feeling increasingly isolated.

She did not want to let him go.

Three

DRESSING UP TIME

I n October, 1988, Modesto Cunanan announced to his wife and son that he wanted to sell their house and move back to the Philippines to try and start afresh. He'd just been fired from his stockbroker job and saw absolutely no reason for staying on in California.

What he didn't tell them was that he had been dismissed from his job for "misappropriating" $106,000 from the business, MaryAnn would later complain in court papers.

It was a big shock for the family as Modesto had been well paid and they'd enjoyed a very comfortable lifestyle.

MaryAnn Cunanan was appalled by her husband's decision and begged him to change his mind. She had absolutely no intention of leaving California.

Modesto—always a quiet and shy character—said he would be unlikely to alter his plans, but they should sell the house anyway and find somewhere smaller and cheaper so they could survive until he moved to the Philippines.

Andrew Cunanan, now just nineteen years old, was not as surprised as his mother was by this hastily announced plan. He had actually been instrumental in encouraging his father to start a new life because he knew from their conversations that he was deeply unhappy living in California.

Modesto Cunanan took his son's encouragement as a definite sign that it was time he made some drastic changes to his life.

Having found a family to buy the Cunanan house in Rancho Bernardo, Modesto Cunanan then insisted he was leaving for the Philippines before the sale was completed. But he assured his wife that there would be enough money left from the deal to pay for MaryAnn to buy a new home and continue to live her accustomed middle-class existence in San Diego.

As if to prove what a turnaround there had been in the relationship between father and son, Modesto even asked Andrew if he wanted to go out and live in Manila.

Cunanan hesitated because he felt a certain loyalty toward his mother. But he was sorely tempted; he had grown bored of the San Diego gay scene. It was small and rumor-driven and Cunanan was so well known in the Hillcrest district that he couldn't have a cup of coffee without the whole town knowing about it.

Modesto Cunanan pressed his son for a decision and then the two of them decided that Cunanan should stay on in California until the house sale was completed and then fly out to the Philippines.

Neither of them seemed concerned by Andrew's college commitments. Cunanan actually couldn't wait to escape school, where his grades were dropping rapidly.

A few days after seeing his father off on a Philippines Airways flight at Los Angeles International Airport, the sale of the house in Rancho Bernardo finally went through. But the vast profit that Modesto Cunanan had promised did not materialize.

It turned out that after lawyers' and real estate fees there was just $3,000 left from the sale for the family to live on.

MaryAnn Cunanan was furious, bitter, and very hurt by her husband's deception. He had effectively abandoned his family and left them virtually destitute. He did eventually send her his $900-a-month Navy pension, but it barely covered their existence.

She vented much of her anger on her "baby" son Andrew whom she felt had become much too close to her husband during the previous few months. To Cunanan it seemed that MaryAnn believed that he had colluded with her husband to betray her. She became convinced that her husband had confided in his son about the real financial situation.

"It got real difficult for Andrew. His mom would shout at him all the time. She seemed to hate him," says San Diego family friend Jean Trenolt.

One day—shortly after Modesto's departure—Cunanan's relationship with his mother reached a nasty boiling point. "MaryAnn rounded on Andrew about being gay. It was the first time they had ever talked about it openly and she was real nasty about it," added Jean Trenolt.

MaryAnn told Cunanan she was ashamed of him and had been ever since she saw him with that man on a San Diego street months earlier.

Cunanan was devastated by his mother's remark. He hesitated and just looked at her for a moment then a dark expression came over his face. Then he stepped forward and slammed her against a wall in the back yard so hard that he dislocated her shoulder.

One neighbor actually saw the attack. "It was very violent but also very quick and Andrew was full of remorse but it was clear that he really hated his mother in many ways. She had smothered him for too long," that same neighbor later explained.

Cunanan was upset by the confrontation. He could cope with most things, but he knew he was wrong to hurt his mother in such a way. He was deeply ashamed about attacking her because that just hadn't been his way of dealing with things.

Looking for a way out he took the easy option and escaped

to the Philippines to see his father. MaryAnn told him in no uncertain terms that she didn't care if she ever saw him again.

The showdown with his mother was a real shock because Cunanan had always been her favorite. MaryAnn was deeply hurt by his decision to move. After all, it was her influence that helped Cunanan to be charming, polite, and sociable in the hope it would lead to a more glamorous life than she could provide.

Cunanan didn't particularly want to abandon his mother in San Diego but felt he did not have any choice. So just halfway through his freshman year, Cunanan dropped out of school to travel to the Philippines.

But a whole series of nasty surprises lay in store for him when he flew into Manila.

Modesto Cunanan had failed to tell his son exactly what kind of life he was leading in the Philippines. Was there a big enough house for them both? How would they survive financially? None of these and many more questions had even been talked about.

Andrew Cunanan could not believe the conditions under which he found his father living. Modesto did not even bother to meet him at the airport, so Cunanan had to take three buses until he finally reached the address in a little town called Plaridel, just north of Manila.

It turned out to be a shack in the middle of one of the worst slums he had ever seen. Cunanan—used to the clean middle-class streets and neat lawns of Rancho Bernardo— was very upset. He was an immaculately clean character and being expected to wash in a ditch and bathe once a week at the local public swimming pool was no joke.

Cunanan then discovered that his father was barely making a living selling junk on street corners. He expected his sensitive nineteen-year-old son to start work with him within hours of his arrival in the Philippines.

Cunanan almost immediately realized he'd made a monumental mistake. He desperately needed to find a way to make enough money to buy a plane ticket back to California.

To make matters worse, he found it virtually impossible to indulge in any romances because most of the men he met emitted bad body odor.

"It was ghastly. I felt so frustrated," Cunanan later told one friend in San Diego.

When Cunanan heard that certain bars were frequented by U.S. Navy sailors, he spruced himself up and spent an entire evening stalking a group of naval ratings in the hope one of them might pick him up. None of them even gave him a second glance.

"Andrew later told me he ended up in some seedy club filled with the filthiest old men. He said it was horrible," recalled a friend from San Diego.

The only good thing about living with his father in the Philippines was that he could reinvent himself with even more frequency than normal. Cunanan actually bounced many of his most outrageous lies around in bars to test them out on unsuspecting Filipinos.

Eventually he found himself a regular gay bar where at least the drinks were reasonably priced and the customers half clean.

Cunanan also became fascinated by the vast number of transsexuals and transvestites who regularly visited such establishments. Up until this point the nearest Cunanan had ever come to this world was to occasionally wear mascara. Certainly there were a few drag queens in San Diego, but he'd rarely come across any of them.

Cunanan soon got to know a number of these so-called girl-boys. He found some of them very attractive and they convinced him that he had just the right features to try cross-dressing. Typically, Cunanan was game for anything. He was bored and felt very strong sexual urges.

He was also completely broke. The girl-boys told Cunanan he could make some easy money by sleeping with men. It wasn't a whole lot different from what he'd been up to in San Diego so Cunanan decided to give it a try.

From then on, at least three times a week—without his father's knowledge—Cunanan spent hours applying makeup, shaving his entire body and styling his hair into a short bob. Then he'd squeeze himself into a skirt and blouse, usually over tights finished off with high pumps.

He even got one of his new boy/girl friends to take photographs of him dressed up as a woman. Later, back in San Diego, he proudly showed the pictures to friends.

"Andrew looked OK, although his features were very heavy, so you pretty well knew he was a boy from the start," explained one old friend.

But that didn't seem to put off any prospective customers.

Cunanan quickly set himself up with regular clients among a group of foreign residents in Manila. They mainly consisted of Spanish, Italian, and English diplomats. He spoke all three languages by this time.

He even proudly told a friend back in San Diego that he had picked up a sailor while dressed as a woman and committed a sex act with the man who never even realized Cunanan was a male.

But Cunanan eventually grew weary of the red-light scene in Manila when groups of armed pimps tried to take control of him. He was banned from many of the traditional pickup joints and reduced to hanging around street corners in the hope of some casual "business."

And many of his clients treated him brutally. They were cold toward him. He was just easy, fresh young meat. That bothered Cunanan in some ways although he also found it exciting because there was little else to do.

But Cunanan longed to be back in San Diego hanging round with all the fat-cat older men. They treated him with respect and ensured he got into all the right places.

Andrew Cunanan couldn't quite believe how low his life had become. He was virtually all alone in a strange country selling his body for a few dollars at a time to anyone willing to pay. California seemed a million miles away.

Despite the extra income from his sex-for-sale activities, Cunanan was still desperately poor and living in those same squalid conditions in his father's shack on the outskirts of Manila.

But within three months of arriving in the Philippines, Cunanan managed to scrape together enough cash to pay for a one-way ticket back to California. His father didn't seem to care whether he went or stayed.

Cunanan had heard from friends in San Diego that his mother was broke. But that wasn't his problem.

Cunanan's relationship with MaryAnn Cunanan had reached an all-time low just before he left for the Philippines and he had no intention of rekindling her love. The two had not even exchanged letters since his departure from California.

In the long, dark sleepless hours he'd spent in that shack on the outskirts of Manila, Cunanan had thought long and hard about his family and concluded he would definitely be better off without them.

Four

THE GOOD, THE BAD,
AND THE UGLY

The Castro district of San Francisco lies quite a way south of the downtown area—a position that makes it the hottest and sunniest part of the city, usually managing to avoid the fogs that blanket most of the rest of San Francisco during the summer.

Perhaps it is therefore rather fitting that Castro is considered the respectable face of gay San Francisco. The small area, filling a few blocks along Castro Street between Market and Twentieth Street, consists of shops and services run entirely by gay men—many of whom are derisively known to the rest of the city as "Castro Clones" for their monotonous haircuts and coitture.

By the spring of 1989, the AIDS crisis had already taken its toll on this spirited community, and much of the busy and often anonymous promiscuity that was a byword for the 1970s had ground to a halt.

Nonetheless the bars and cafes of Castro were ample proof that gay men were still the best party-goers on any circuit.

It was into this cosmopolitan, carefree atmosphere that Andrew Cunanan stepped following a brief stay in San Diego after his troubled return from the Philippines.

Cunanan had always longed to stay in the Castro district, having heard so much about it from his gay friends back in the Hillcrest area of San Diego.

When he arrived in the city he knew he had to put on his most charming characterization if he were going to find a companion to keep him in the style he had become accustomed to before he left for the Philippines.

Cunanan was armed with numerous phone numbers of gay associates who'd come through San Diego and he hoped to infiltrate a pleasant social scene as rapidly as possible.

In the daytime he loved wandering up and down Harvey Milk Plaza, dedicated to the gay supervisor who before his assassination in 1978 owned a camera store and was a popular figure in the Castro.

Cunanan also liked to walk down the hill from the plaza toward the junction of Castro and Eighteenth Street, which marked the area's epicenter and was cluttered with book shops, clothing stores, cafes, and bars.

At first, Cunanan found it difficult to break into the Castro district's tightly knit gay social scene. People proved unreliable at calling him back and he was surprised by how many men seemed rather reluctant to meet a stranger, despite the recommendations of others.

Cunanan had taken a cheap room in a boarding house just off Castro Street and decided he would have to bide his time. He had a few savings and he wanted to find the perfect suitor to improve the quality of his life.

He also began putting his favorite hobby to the test once more—reinventing himself.

In the Badlands Bar, in Castro, Cunanan frequently posed as a naval officer on leave. "Lieutenant Commander Cummings" became known in Badlands as a good hand at performing magic tricks for other patrons. With his immaculate haircut, bulging biceps, and all-over tan he soon became a very popular figure.

Cunanan had actually fine-tuned his magical skills during hours of boredom on the cluttered streets of Manila. A man who was one of his father's neighbors had taught him some rudimentary tricks. Now those skills were proving a pleasant diversion from the tedium of waiting for the perfect partner to come into his life.

Part of Cunanan's reinvention routine was also to carefully and deliberately blend the characteristics of friends, lovers, and family members into fanciful brews, then claim those people's lives as his own.

It was an ideal escape mode for a young man whose life had deteriorated drastically since those heady, happy days at private school in San Diego.

Regulars at Badlands were particularly impressed that "Lieutenant Cummings" refused all offers of a free drink from other patrons. "He actually didn't drink and only smoked the occasional cigar," said one member of the bar staff. "He wasn't on the make at all."

But then Cunanan knew only too well that wealthy older men would shy away from any young guys they thought were just after their money. He wanted to attract just the right kind of suitor. For Andrew Cunanan it was a plain and simple case of survival. There was no other way.

In other bars along the Castro strip, Cunanan reinvented himself as Andrew DeSilva—his favorite name of all—or sometimes simply "Andy." Other more Latino names are also recalled by members of staff still working in those establishments to this day.

Cunanan's chameleonlike qualities were his trademark because no one in any of those bars realized that Andrew Cunanan/DeSilva/Cummings was the same person. To some he was a studious-looking character in horn-rimmed glasses, to others he was a suave tuxedoed charmer who spoke of his friends in high places.

The only giveaway might have been his eyes—dark and moody, often narrowed in an angry squint. But for months in San Francisco no one realized that all these characters were the same person.

Cunanan even took a lowly job as a kitchen worker in a restaurant to make ends meet. But on his nights off he'd be found lording it up in some bar or club regaling men with tales about himself being the owner of thousands of acres of prime land on the French Riviera or heir to a sugar plantation or the scion of a wealthy Jewish family.

Cunanan was getting to the point where he was pretending to be other people more often than he was being himself.

He liked to invent new versions of his life story, depending on what type of people he was hanging out with. Sometimes he could be an aspiring actor called Christopher. Other times he was the successful owner of a construction company.

Cunanan was brilliant at judging the type of story that would be convincing to a certain kind of person.

One time he even admitted to one of the few friends in the Castro district who actually knew his real identity, "Everyone has their own version of what they think I am. Nobody knows the truth."

And that was the way Cunanan liked to keep it. He felt a strange sense of inner security by not giving away any of the real secrets of his life.

Cunanan was enjoying his stay in San Francisco despite his failure to find a wealthy older man and continued to date other, younger, more energetic men. One of them was an architect called David Madson.

The two met in a San Francisco restaurant and immediately embarked on a passionate but brief affair. But Madson, a handsome Midwesterner in his mid-twenties, was concerned by certain aspects of Cunanan's character.

Madson questioned whether the sources of Cunanan's income were legal. He also became suspicious because Cunanan wouldn't give out an address or telephone number to his new friend. He suspected Cunanan was into drugs rather than prostitution.

In the end the relationship fizzled out and Madson later

told one close friend, Rich Bonnin, from Minneapolis, that he had been worried by Cunanan "because he seemed to be hiding so many secrets."

By the time Halloween came around in 1989, Cunanan was supplementing his income by some smalltime marijuana dealing and occasionally sleeping for money with men he met in bars. He was actually more discrete about the drug dealing than the illicit sex.

It wasn't full-fledged prostitution like in Manila. Instead, he would allow himself to be picked up and then casually "suggest" to his brief encounters that they might like to pay for his cab home. Most men were happy to pay a few hundred dollars out for such a handsome partner.

On a couple of occasions, Cunanan struck gold when he was paid a thousand bucks to spend the night with men, but those opportunities were extremely rare.

Cunanan was transfixed by the colorful Halloween celebrations in the Castro district that year. It was the zenith of the social calender when inhibitions died and every gay in town seemed to be out on the sidewalks to watch six-foot transvestite beauties bedecked in jewels and ballgowns strutting noisily between the Cafe San Marcos and The Elephant Walk, two of the Castro's most popular watering holes.

Cunanan—wearing just shorts and sneakers—was fascinated by the display and worked his way into a group of middle-aged men out for a stroll among the heaving crowds. All around him men were kissing and sometimes even more.

The police—who had blocked off roads to keep the carnival floats moving—turned a blind eye to all such minor indiscretions.

Cunanan later told a friend that he had group sex with the men he met that day and that one of them—an older man—wanted more than just a casual fling. He also proudly claimed to friends that he was a well known TV actor. Cunanan had at last struck gold.

However Cunanan didn't want to make it too easy for this older man at first. He deliberately played it cool so as to ensure his new partner became completely besotted by the younger, handsome, dark-haired twenty-year-old.

It was all part of the games that his mother had taught him to play all those years earlier in San Diego. Once again her advice was being put to use. Andrew Cunanan had no intention of struggling along as a casual kitchen worker forever.

Within weeks, he and this older man had become very close and Cunanan was "persuaded" to move into a house in the nearby Berkeley district with his new partner, who told his friends and associates that Cunanan was his new secretary and would be living at the property indefinitely.

As Californian writer and Cunanan associate Nicole Ramirez Murray would later explain: "He led a double life. One among the wealthy closet cases and the wealthy prominent businessmen. And another with his peers—a bar social life. He would pick up the tab and be the life of the party.

"He was the perfect American gigolo. He was suave, and he obviously fed his brain. The arts, the opera, antiques, museums.

"Usually these guys can only talk about the gym and the surf. They are like GQ models. He was the least handsome, the least built. But he knew how to keep these older gentlemen interested. He knew how to give them a conversation."

Cunanan couldn't believe his luck in finding such a perfect partner. But then he had just the right image to attract older men.

"The strange thing about him was his normality," explained old acquaintance Anthony White. "He dressed real mainstream conservative—khaki pants and a plaid shirt.

That's what made him so attractive to older, more discrete guys."

Another associate from Cunanan's stay in San Francisco explained: "The older, richer guys tend to be real conservative. They don't want some girly guy who prances around. They want a guy who looks so normal he might be straight and Andy fitted that bill perfectly."

At the Midnight Star bar in the Castro district, manager Jesse Cappachionse found Cunanan "a bit enigmatic." He later explained: "He was always good at blending in with people. He was always near the center of the bar, always the center of attention, but I don't think anybody knew him very well."

Cunanan was very careful not to let his sleazier "other side"—the cross dressing and gay prostitution come out. He was greatly helped in this by his propensity for adopting different guises whenever he frequented bars in the Castro district.

Cunanan's new live-in lover also introduced his diligently well-mannered young escort to a different kind of San Francisco social scene from the gay bars and leather clubs in the Castro.

The "couple" became regular patrons at the San Francisco Opera House and Cunanan found himself mixing with interior decorators, designers, architects, and even movie stars such as Robin Williams.

But old habits die hard.

Cunanan also continued to enjoy dating other, younger, more energetic men.

In October, 1990, Cunanan and his older, regular lover visited a party held in Stars restaurant for a reception following the opera *Capriccio*. He was to meet someone who would feature prominently in his life almost seven years later.

Fashion designer Gianni Versace was well known in San Francisco for sweeping into town with some handsome young man or other on his arm.

Old friend Jeremiah Tower never forgot his first meeting with the Italian designer.

"It was as Versace and a young guy were trying to enter the Clift Hotel without a jacket or tie. The manager stepped forward to usher them out and I came to the rescue."

Tower continued: "I said to the manager, 'Between the two of them, they have about $40,000 in clothes on.' Versace was dressed in the most perfect Versace you've ever seen, and his companion was dressed in perfect Versace leather."

Realizing whom he was dealing with, the manager eventually relented.

Andrew Cunanan was introduced to the flamboyant Versace in the lobby of Stars restaurant following the opera. The two men shook hands politely. Versace said he thought they had met before at his house in Lake Como. Cunanan didn't disagree since he'd visited that area of Italy with an older lover a couple of years previously. It seemed a pleasant enough talking point.

Cunanan also couldn't resist showing off his fluent Italian to the Milan-based fashion guru. Versace seemed impressed, but their conversation was interrupted by numerous others wanting to pay homage to the designer.

Later, Cunanan breathlessly told anyone who would listen about his meeting with Versace. He was proud of meeting the designer and talked about him as if he were a friend even though they hardly knew each other.

That same evening, Cunanan went to a reception at the gay nightclub Colossus. The place was filled with drag queens, men dressed as mini-skirted, roller-skating nuns, and gay bikers wearing leather shorts and bondage masks. Across the crowd he spotted his hero Versace dancing with a handsome young male-model type.

He went up and tried to talk to Versace, but the designer's surrounding entourage and the noise of the music made it virtually impossible to carry on a proper conversation. In the end they just shrugged shoulders at each other and Cunanan eventually moved off.

In the early hours of the following morning, after Versace had left the premises, Cunanan bumped into an old acquaintance called Erik Gruenwald. He told him the exciting news: "I just met Gianni Versace."

Gruenwald replied: "Sure, and I'm Coco Chanel."

Meeting people of the stature of Gianni Versace simply fed Andrew Cunanan with even more of a taste for the good life—and he liked it immensely. By manipulating men he was starting to discover what it was like to be a member of the gay jetset.

But not long after that meeting with Versace he also discovered that beneath the glitz and glamor lay a seedy underbelly of sexual deviancy that was the price he was expected to pay for being allowed into this exclusive world.

Five

SEX LIVES AND VIDEOTAPE

According to Woody Allen, California's only worthwhile contribution to society was allowing right turns on a red light. But Andrew Cunanan certainly wouldn't have agreed with that assessment.

He was living a lavish lifestyle in San Francisco and enjoying every minute of excess.

However there was a price to pay—although it didn't seem to bother Cunanan all that much.

For he had rapidly discovered that sadistic sexual habits prevailed even among the most elite of San Francisco's gay population.

The city overflowed with nightlife in the early 1990s. But it was a labyrinthine in the extreme, with a very serious sadomasochistic community, a body piercing epidemic, and a lot more besides.

Cunanan entered this underworld maze through his new set of friends and sometimes, when they were bored, he and his older lover would flick through a copy of *The Spectator*—bought from thousands of vending machines throughout the city—and check the club listings. There were also the numerous fetish clothes shops, where flyers could be easily picked up.

Cunanan and his lover became regulars at leather and

rubber stores like Mr. S. Leather, described as a "leatherman's paradise" by its owner.

Cunanan and his partner's favorite clubs featured names that made their intentions loud and clear: Bondage a Go-Go, Hellbound and Sodom.

Many private parties were held in real dungeons where bondage equipment was available for any guests to use. At these events, often called "play parties" anyone was welcome so long as they bought whips and chains and were prepared to strap their lover to any of the apparatus.

When Cunanan allowed a heavy leather bullwhip to be used on him one night he almost suffered very severe damage to his kidneys.

He then discovered that in San Francisco, the main "weapon" of choice was a multitailed cat, or "flogger" as it was known among the gay community. The handle was robust, interleaved with black or colored leather strips.

Soon Cunanan was allowing his lover to deliver blows with it on his bare back. At first he just lay there and took it, but gradually he began to enjoy the sensation. This was when his appetite for such twisted sexual games first properly developed. But there was more to come.

The game of relationships between the master and his sexual slave are subtle and delicate. Sex slaves are expected to know how to indicate the limits to the masters so as not to exceed them. Absolute authority was the name of the game that Andrew Cunanan was already discovering.

The slightest false step would break the harmony and shatter the relationship he had with his older partner.

Cunanan hadn't been surprised when his lover suggested they take part in sadomasochistic games. He admitted how he had often been to some of the leather bars on Castro—and on one occasion had been back to a man's apartment and allowed him to divulge in his fantasies. He also mentioned those two or three experiences back in San Diego.

Cunanan's latest lover was obviously very involved in the "scene" and wanted Cunanan to regularly allow himself to be beaten.

He also persuaded Cunanan—with little effort—to star in two graphic, low-budget sadomasochistic gay pornographic videos, which are still in circulation in San Francisco to this day. Cunanan was paid nothing for appearing in these videos. He did it to keep his lover happy and because he wanted to find out what it would be like to have sex in such a public setting.

"Andrew said he really enjoyed making those porno flicks. But they were pretty heavy, although he talked about them as if they were some form of art," recalled a gay friend in San Diego.

In both the hardcore videos, Cunanan played the role to which he had already become accustomed—the sex slave. In one of the most disturbing scenes he was psychically tortured and abused by a gang of men in a mass rape scene that even the most hardened of Cunanan's friends found difficult to watch.

"It was sick stuff but Andy just kept saying, 'It's only acting. It's only acting.' He knew some of us disapproved," added one friend.

Cunanan was well aware that all human beings had their limits, but he felt he couldn't point this out to his regular San Francisco partner for fear it might ruin their very convenient relationship. In any case, his lover made it clear that he expected there to be few boundaries between them, morally or physically. The danger was that some of these deviations might prove fatal.

By all accounts, Cunanan did not find it very difficult to adhere to the role of sex slave because he had a clear motive for adapting to the demands of another person. His mother had taught him how to charm people and then appear to concede things when it was necessary to get what he wanted. This was just another version of that.

As a slave he was expected to grant his partner—his master in the relationship—the privileges of his function: to allow him to dominate him. To be obedient down to the last command.

Cunanan's partner insisted that he should look on their experiences as an art form. Cunanan wasn't so convinced, but he believed the games they played behind closed doors hinged on the strength of their relationship, so he allowed himself to be physically and mentally abused.

Sometimes other men were introduced to the scene, much to Cunanan's dislike. He saw them as threats to his continued relationship with his older lover.

Cunanan's induction into this disturbing world of sexual depravity had other spinoffs. Now the fantasies he had been harboring for so long were going to be turned into reality. Basically, he would do just about anything to stay in control of his own destiny even though, ironically, this included allowing himself to be subjected to degrading acts of sexual perversion.

But the images of the discipline he endured at the hands of his father kept coming back to haunt him and he didn't like such painful reminders.

By 1992, life in San Francisco had reached its peak for Andrew Cunanan. He had swapped one middle-aged partner for another, richer, man.

This time Cunanan was even given a credit card to use whenever he wanted. Cunanan was soon entertaining his younger gay companions to lavish meals at some of San Francisco's most expensive restaurants.

By this time Cunanan's interest in sadomasochism had developed into his own regular addiction. He often bought gay rubber and leather glossy magazines and would flick through them with his lover or when he was alone and bored. He kept a drawer full of sex toys that he was always trying to persuade partners to use. He also had rubber underwear and trousers that he sometimes wore when he was out cruising the local gay bars.

Cunanan's interest in such paraphernalia was in many ways fed by his boredom. He no longer had to work because he was a kept man, but while his lover was out working he found himself drifting through the days, his head filled with lurid fantasies.

Inevitably, that last relationship eventually fizzled out. Cunanan saw that as an indication it was time to go back to San Diego and see his old friends. San Francisco had been a highly profitable adventure, but he felt he could retain more control over his life by going back to old, familiar territory.

Once back in the predominantly gay Hillside district, Cunanan quickly linked up with his old acquaintances and regaled them with tales of his adventures in San Francisco and Manila.

And, perhaps not so surprisingly, Cunanan's old habits continued to dominate his life. Within days of getting a small shared apartment in Hillside, he was dating an older, richer man.

Anthony White, a waiter at the California Cuisine restaurant, in Hillside, saw Cunanan often come in during this period in the company of older men.

"He'd usually pay the bill for everyone and sometimes it came to as much as $1,000," White said. "He didn't have that subservient attitude you'd expect from a kept boy."

Despite his new relationship, Cunanan continued to dance regularly at hard rock bars frequented by young professionals and off-duty servicemen. He'd often be seen leaving on the arm of yet another man.

Another of his San Diego friends, Mike Whitmore, noticed

that Cunanan made a point of giving the clear impression he was a likeable, easygoing guy.

"I'd known him for five or six years. He always seemed to keep his cool. He was very personable. Always had a crowd of friends around him," Whitmore later said.

But Whitmore became aware there was another side to his friend.

"He was always very secretive about his past and where the money came from. He insinuated that his family had a great deal of money and that's where it came from. He was definitely very mysterious."

There was even talk that Cunanan's latest rich patron paid him $2,000 a month for sex on demand. The man—like one of his earlier lovers—even took Cunanan to New York and Europe.

Meanwhile Andrew Cunanan continued to work the bars and clubs easily, picking up younger men whose physical company he desired. It was a fantasy lifestyle away from the mundane problems of everyday life in the real world.

But, as always, Cunanan would once again soon discover that there was a high price to pay for such a debauched existence.

In the summer of 1992, Andrew Cunanan surprised many of his gay friends and associates in the Hillcrest district of San Diego by moving back in with his mother MaryAnn.

Cunanan paid half the rent on a condo they shared near the center of San Diego. They both struck up a no-questions-asked agreement over Cunanan's nighttime habits, which involved frequent absences from the apartment.

MaryAnn Cunanan was in a virtual state of denial about her son's sexual preferences and continued trying to convince him to attend the local Catholic church with her.

One relative later explained: "MaryAnn attended church most days and on a few occasions Andrew even went with her. But I think he was only doing it to please her.''

Cunanan continued to be incredibly open about his homosexuality with everyone he met—apart from his family.

The relative went on: ''We all realized he was gay but he never came out and said it openly to us. But many of us heard about his relationships through friends and associates. It was the most open of secrets. But we respected the fact he didn't want to embarrass us by talking about it.''

Back in the Hillcrest district, Cunanan seemed anything but embarrassed.

John Belman, who encountered Cunanan on numerous occasions found Cunanan's charms often exceeded the sum of his parts, but that he was able to converse on diverse topics and in different languages.

''He could charm the birds from the trees and he seemed to possess genuine intellect,'' Belman later recalled.

And Cunanan continued to pretend to be just about anyone when the mood took his fancy. Many members of the Hillcrest community knew he was a Walter Mitty-type character, but they decided that was just part of his charm.

At this time his favorite reinvention was to call himself Lieutenant Commander Cummings, of Choate and Yale, importer of antiques. He even wore blazers and ascots and smoked Cohiba cigars.

Cunanan was deliberately cultivating an aristocratic manner because he was convinced that it would help him snag richer companions.

When he wanted to be a stronger, tall dark stranger type he'd call himself Curt Matthews DeMaris. The names had to fit the tasks at hand.

One of Cunanan's favorite hangouts in Hillcrest was a restaurant called California Cuisine, located along a stretch of bars and boutiques among the city's lively gay enclave.

Manager George Kalamaras later recalled, ''We knew him

as such a mild-mannered person. Charming, reserved, and classy.''

At Flicks, a gay video bar along a stretch of University Avenue, in Hillcrest, owner Tim Burthel got to know Cunanan well as he would often wander into the bar and watch the small screen shows of beach parties featuring well-oiled, well-muscled men. Interestingly, Burthal gained a completely different impression of Cunanan.

''He was kind of snobby and always had a lot of money,'' said Burthal.

But that perfectly summed up Cunanan. Rich and sophisticated as ''Lt. Cummings.'' Quiet and shy as plain ''Andy.''

Often, Cunanan would sit down at the Flicks bar and peel off hundred dollar bills from huge wads of cash to buy drinks for anyone he befriended. He regularly bragged about his associations with the rich and famous, including people like fashion designer Gianni Versace.

He also regularly turned up in expensive cars, which led many of his acquaintances to presume he probably had more than one sugar daddy supporting him.

However, one day at Flicks Bar, Cunanan threw all this into confusion by pulling a creased photograph of a woman and baby out of his pocket and announcing that it was his ex-wife and child.

''I don't think anyone believed him,'' Flicks owner Tim Barthal explained later. ''He seemed to want to make himself seem more worldly, more experienced, like he'd done it all.''

Many of Cunanan's friends and associates in Hillcrest were convinced that Cunanan was pretending to have a wife and newborn baby so that it would make him even more of a challenge to any prospective sexual partner.

''Some gay men are turned on by the thought of 'converting' a straight guy and I reckon Andrew was using this family routine as a way of trying to make himself more sexy in the eyes of certain guys,'' explained one of his old Hillcrest friends.

But Cunanan insisted that they could not have been more wrong.

Six

CRUISE CONTROL

A ndrew Cunanan maintained that he met and secretly married a young Spanish woman in 1994. A bizarre marriage by anyone's standards. This was the story he would tell:

Cunanan had been approached in a gay bar by a man he knew and asked if he would be prepared to marry the woman so she could get a green card and stay in the U.S. His fee would be $1,000 cash.

Ever the opportunist when it came to money, Cunanan agreed without hesitation.

As a young, fit, preppy-looking type it was reckoned that no one would be suspicious of Cunanan's motives because he looked so heterosexual.

So, Cunanan went ahead with the marriage in San Diego and the "happy couple" took their vows, went for a brief drink with friends at a local bar and then exchanged a kiss on each cheek before saying their good-byes.

That would have been the end of Cunanan's "marriage" if he hadn't bumped into the girl about two months later in a San Diego street.

Explained San Diego friend Henry Brunt: "Andy told me later that he actually felt quite attracted to this woman. She was very dark and Latin-looking. I guess it was the way he wanted to look when he dressed as a woman."

Cunanan went on a couple of dates with the girl and they got on famously. Then they slept together and she immediately got pregnant.

Cunanan—who'd always been fascinated by the idea of bisexuality although he'd insisted to friends he wasn't "bi"—was completely caught by surprise.

His friend continued: "Andy panicked. He wanted her to have an abortion at first, but the girl got very emotional."

Cunanan's "wife" refused to even consider an abortion because of her strict Catholic upbringing—which Cunanan fully appreciated.

But his dilemma was that he couldn't afford to bring up mother and child without the support of his elderly sugar daddies, whom he relied on for financial backing.

The girl pleaded with Cunanan to get a proper job to support them.

Cunanan agreed to give it a try and took on the only recorded legitimate job he ever had in San Diego—as a clerk in a Thrifty Drug Store in the city.

To Cunanan it was the ultimate insult to have to work such a lowly position. He even got into the habit of always wearing his glasses and becoming very dowdy in appearance in the store in the hope that none of his acquaintances would recognize him working as a clerk.

After less than a month he quit his job and told his "wife" the only way he could survive was to continue seeking out financial support from older gay men.

Cunanan never considered the health risk he had exposed his wife to by sleeping with her and continuing his homosexual relationships elsewhere.

By the time baby was born, Cunanan and his wife had parted.

Cunanan later described the relationship as the biggest mistake of his life. "I'm gay and I'll never fight it again," he told one friend.

Cunanan would never experiment with women again. He'd seen the misery of his parents' life together and that would always drive him away from a traditional domestic relationship.

However Cunanan said he did occasionally make contact with his wife and he even sent mother and child some money whenever he could afford it.

But contact between them faded out some years later when she officially divorced Cunanan and remarried.

At the tidy condo he still shared with his mother, Cunanan never once even admitted to her that he'd had a heterosexual relationship.

MaryAnn's strict Catholicism and rigid habits successfully inhibited her son to such an extent that he still felt he couldn't talk to her about anything of a personal nature.

The apartment was at least a refuge away from the one-night stands, sugar daddies, and lovechild problems. But that was its only attraction to Cunanan.

For his mother continued to lay down the law in other ways. She kept hassling him to go to church more. She would occasionally try and find out where he was getting his money from. Cunanan would immediately clam up. It simply added to the tension in the household.

Eventually MaryAnn's attitude began to convince Cunanan he had to quickly find a proper full-time partner who could fully support him so he could get away from his mother.

MaryAnn Cunanan had become so twisted up in knots about her son's homosexuality that there were times when you could cut through the atmosphere in the apartment with a knife. On those occasions, Cunanan would storm out, go to a gay club and pick up a man, virtually any man he could lay his hands on.

"MaryAnn was an introverted, deeply religious woman who buried her thoughts and feelings in Catholicism. It was all she lived for," explained one relative.

"But she needed Andrew's contribution toward the rent in order to survive so she had no choice but to continue to allow him to live at the condo. And I guess in her own way she loved him."

One day near the end of 1995, Cunanan announced to his mother that he would be moving out of their condo because he had landed a full-time job as the live-in secretary to a millionaire businessman called Norman Blachford, who owned a large oceanfront condo in the nearby resort of La Jolla.

MaryAnn was upset. Her husband had stopped sending his $900-a-month navy pension, and she was facing destitution. Cunanan didn't really care. He just wanted to get away from her.

Cunanan was immensely relieved when MaryAnn announced she intended to move up to Eureka, Illinois, to settle in a public housing apartment. She'd also be near another son, Christopher.

In La Jolla, things were looking up for Cunanan. Norman Blachford—a semiretired businessman in his late sixties—immediately gave Cunanan a dark green Infiniti and a monthly allowance of $2,500.

Blachford was an Arizona philanthropist and major contributor to the Phoenix Symphony Orchestra. Cunanan and Blachford were soon to be regularly seen together at symphony functions.

La Jolla was the perfect oceanside resort for Andrew Cunanan to recharge his batteries. He'd spent the previous year involved in brutal, often short-term relationships that had sapped his spirit. He wanted this new relationship to provide him with more stability—and a lot more financial clout.

The main street of La Jolla—Prospect—felt like something from the Cote d'Azur, with dozens of good restaurants offering all types of cuisine. Behind it, dazzling whitewashed homes were tucked neatly into the hillside overlooking the Pacific Ocean.

Only seventy years earlier, La Jolla had once been known as nothing more than a tent city, where farmers let their cattle wander onto the beaches, and, according to some of the more elderly residents, "You were up to your ankles in dust during the summer and up to your ankles in mud during the winter."

But times had changed and in the thirties, La Jolla had been designated as an upmarket resort town that prided itself on being separate from San Diego, just a few miles to the south. In fact, La Jolla had become such an orderly society in the fifties, that residents had even insisted on giving their houses names rather than numbers.

A few years before Andrew Cunanan turned up in the town, resident Betty Broderick gave La Jolla the sort of reputation it could well have done without when she murdered her husband and his new wife in a case that became infamous through America.

Cunanan and his partner Norman soon became regular visitors to the beach and restaurants such as Vic's Fisherman's Grill, on Fay Avenue, tucked just off Prospect Street.

Cunanan and his older companion also went on expensive trips to Europe. Paris was their favorite city.

La Jolla waiter Jim Allen remembered them both, but it was Cunanan who seemed the more interesting of the two.

"Andrew always had a special air about him. 'Out of my way—I'm really busy right now. I'm wearing very expensive clothes.' He had one of those large, checkbook-size wallets. He'd open it, and you'd see rows of platinum credit cards. They were all in his name."

They'd all been given to him by Norman Blachford.

But the lure of nearby Hillcrest, in San Diego, soon proved too much for Cunanan. Whenever Norman was away on business trips he would slip into the nearby city and turn up at all his favorite old gay haunts.

At one stage he even started a relationship with another wealthy, elderly man—a San Diego architect named Lincoln Aston. The friendship was only known to a handful of Cunanan's friends because he knew that Blachford would drop him like a stone if he found out Cunanan had been dating another older man.

Associates say the relationship with Aston ended suddenly and Cunanan never fully explained why.

Lincoln Aston was found beaten to death with a stone obelisk in 1995. It wasn't until more than a year later that a mentally retarded drifter walked into a Colorado police station and insisted he'd committed the killing.

In San Diego, Cunanan was still famous for picking up the tab in Hillcrest's restaurants, bars, and clubs. Often he'd buy round after round of drinks as well as dinner. Those bills would frequently be in the region of $1,000. One of his favorite haunts was Top of the Park, a neighborhood spot known as a prime meeting place for wealthy gay men in town.

But the strangest thing about Cunanan was that he never appeared in Hillcrest with a date on his arm. Instead, he'd find a new friend, start plying them with drinks and then attract a crowd.

Cunanan often found himself surrounded by many men sponging drinks off him. Yet later he'd often complain to friends that many of them weren't interested in going out on a date. Cunanan expected people to live by the same rules as him. He believed that money would buy him anything he wanted, including casual relationships.

In late 1995, Cunanan's relationship with Norman Blachford took a turn for the worse. The older man was increasingly fed up at the large amounts of money his lover was spending on other men in the bars and clubs of the Hillcrest district. They split up.

Typically, Cunanan announced to his friend Michael Williams: "I'm not going to return properly to Norman until he buys me a Mercedes."

Cunanan wasn't actually that bothered about the breakup because he'd met an extremely wealthy interior decorator in his fifties who wanted Cunanan to join him for the summer at his house in the exclusive millionaire's paradise of the Hamptons on the East Coast.

It was a perfect opportunity for Cunanan to escape his problems with Norman Blachford—because he was convinced that the Hamptons would prove an ideal hunting ground for richer, more famous partners. He was always willing and prepared to sell his body in exchange for a lifestyle.

The Hamptons—the fabled Long Island hideaway for New Yorkers with old money—was the city's summer playground. Its little hamlets—Southampton, Bridgehampton, East Hampton, and Sag Habor to name but a few—were havens to which only the very rich flocked.

Despite the events of the past, Cunanan had stopped considering himself to be a male prostitute. He saw himself as an opportunist who happened to be homosexual and was perfectly able to use his body to get exactly what he wanted.

So it was that in the summer of 1996, Cunanan showed up as one of the bright new faces on the gay circuit in the so-called anything-goes Hamptons.

Dozens of immensely rich and powerful men met him at a series of parties and dinners that Cunanan usually turned up at in the company of his older, interior decorator partner-of-the-moment.

However, Cunanan attended one party without his rich

suitor, who had remained back at his vast home near South-ampton.

One of the guests later recalled how impressively Cunanan held his own at the get-together hosted by one of Hollywood's most famous gay producers.

"Andrew was very impressive. He had the ability to look you straight in the eye when he talked to you in such a way that you felt you were the only man for him," said the man.

At this particular party, Cunanan reinvented himself once again as Andrew DeSilva, heir to vast property in the south of France and virtually a member of the Spanish aristocracy. He even claimed he'd done a little acting in Hollywood. It was all just another pipe dream, although Cunanan had tried to set himself up as an actor while in San Diego but no one would take him seriously.

"He was immaculately dressed and had this habit of allowing his hand to brush your leg throughout conversations. I was quite taken by him," added another guest.

That night one of the guests offered Cunanan a ride home.

"I knew the house in which he was staying and I even knew his host pretty well," the man later explained.

During the drive back to Cunanan's partner's home, the twenty-five-year-old proudly showed off a gold Cartier tank watch he said had been given to him by a very special friend.

"I suspected he was a bit of a gigolo," said the other guest. "But it didn't seem to really matter at the time. He obviously had no difficulty insinuating himself into our lives. He was well-dressed, well-spoken, and good looking and he had good taste."

But Cunanan's obsession with being accepted did have a downside.

"The only thing you could say about him was that he was a bit pompous, a bit too pleased with himself," added the party guest.

Cunanan made it clear during the journey that he had met

numerous famous members of the Hamptons' so-called "Velvet Mafia," which included designers, the fashion crowd, Hollywood actors and executives, record people, and major figures in publishing.

The man driving just couldn't tell if he was being serious or not. But he tended to believe him.

Cunanan's stay in the Hamptons lasted less than two months, but during that time he went out of his way to network many of the most famous residents. He was intrigued by many of them and wanted to work out a way to make use of these newfound connections.

Back in San Diego that fall, Cunanan's friends teased him mercilessly about his preferences for older men. He insisted he preferred their company.

"They're more stimulating. More interesting," Cunanan told one friend.

But there was one younger man on the scene who would change the destiny of Andrew Cunanan's life.

Seven

FEVER

J eff Trail was a handsome twenty-six-year-old engineer who had first met Andrew Cunanan in a bar in Coronado, California, back in 1992. Cunanan later told a friend that it was the first time in his life that he'd actually fallen in love with somebody on first sight.

Trail, then a Navy lieutenant, was in many ways a very similar-looking character to Cunanan. He was well built, extremely fit with dark hair and a rugged handsomeness that made his homosexuality quite a surprise to many of the gay men he encountered. He certainly didn't fit the stereotype.

Andrew Cunanan was very taken by Trail, but as always he had his other older, richer man agenda to follow at that time.

Cunanan had wanted a brief sexual encounter with Trail but Trail's unwillingness to enter into such a relationship made him even more attractive to Cunanan.

Cunanan spent a small fortune on his older lovers' credit cards lavishing gifts such as a watch and some jewelry on Trail.

But Trail continued to insist on a purely platonic relationship because he was already attached to someone else.

Cunanan, who knew no such emotional boundaries, was baffled by Trail's loyalty to his partner.

* * *

In reality Cunanan and Trail offered the starkest of contrasts. Cunanan was a man who inflated, embellished, and lied outright about his family background to give it an air of mystery and intrigue. He was flashy, lived life to the edge, and was openly gay.

Trail, meanwhile, had learned to live life with discretion, a trait mandated by the fact he was a gay man who had first established his homosexuality while in the military.

Trail was from a middle-class family in DeKalb. Illinois, and had four brothers and sisters. His father, Stan, was a hardworking family man who brought his children up in a happy, noisy household.

Jeffrey had been an immensely popular and hardworking student at DeKalb High and his favorite extracurricular activity was the speech team.

Before graduating in 1987, Trail won an appointment to the U.S. Naval Academy in Annapolis. He entered the Academy in May, 1987, and graduated in May, 1991, as an ensign. But he stayed at the academy through the summer, serving as a training officer for the plebes, as the freshmen are known.

In October, 1991, Trail entered the Navy's Surface Warfare School in San Diego, and graduated from there the following May. Winning a promotion to lieutenant junior grade, he was assigned to the U.S.S. *Gridley*, a guided missile cruiser in the Pacific Fleet, based in San Diego.

Throughout this time Trail was actually secretly living with another naval officer in a house on the outskirts of the Hillcrest district in San Diego.

Years later, the woman who owned the house, recalled, "Jeffrey was a very friendly, outgoing person. Nice-looking, just a very kind person. If you needed something done, he was there to do it."

Trail and his roommate lived quietly and discretely. After

all, this was before President Clinton's "don't ask, don't tell" policy involving gays in the military. The two officers genuinely feared the Navy would discover their secret and court-martial them.

Trail's roommate was extremely paranoid and nervous about the fact that he and Jeff were living together. However Trail was far more relaxed about the situation.

"He was not the real braggart kind of person. He was a very down to earth, very kind, very gentle person," explained one friend.

It was that gentleness that appealed to Andrew Cunanan. He had been used and abused by so many men in his short life, but in Trail he felt he had found a companion who would love him for what he was.

Trail was such a regular kind of guy. He had a dog, liked listening to Frank Sinatra records, worked out a lot at the gym and enjoyed hiking in the desert and mountains of Central California.

When Cunanan first became attached to Trail, the handsome young naval officer was still living with his Navy roommate. The two men even had dinner parties at the house to which Cunanan and others were asked.

By this time Trail was working as a boiler room engineer on the *Gridley*. But when it was decommissioned in 1994, he was assigned to Assault Craft Unit 1, stationed at the Naval Amphibious Base, at Coronado, near San Diego.

In November, 1995, Trail was promoted to lieutenant. His live-in relationship ended and gradually he became closer to Cunanan, but they were still not sleeping together.

Trail's five-year active duty stint ended in the spring of 1996, and he was given an honorable discharge.

On May 20, 1996, Trail enrolled in the California Highway Patrol Academy, in West Sacramento, California. He was a cadet in class CTC2-96.

At first Trail was so enthusiastic about the job he even

bought his own Remington Peters .40 pistol just like the ones that the CHP used.

Trail and Cunanan would regularly go to a local firing range and shoot the weapon for hours at a time. They were soon both very able marksmen. But Trail noted that Cunanan seemed a little over excited whenever he handled the gun and would wave it around a lot.

"Treat it gently, Andy," Trail told his friend one day. "That's a killing machine you got there, not some toy pop-gun."

But at the real CHP, Jeff Trail rapidly concluded that the life of a highway patrol officer was not for him. Trail joked about not finding the tight-fitting beige uniform "sexy enough" but the truth was that he encountered a lot of homophobia in the academy and felt very isolated.

Officially, the academy recorded that Trail left them on July 23, citing "personal reasons."

Throughout all this he saw a lot of Cunanan, but they still remained just good friends.

By all accounts, Cunanan had even become resigned to the fact that his earlier infatuation with Trail had developed into a genuine friendship.

Shortly after dropping his CHP plans, Trail attended a job fair in San Diego. Among the firms recruiting at the event was Ferrellgas, a propane company based in Liberty, Missouri.

Trail told the firm's recruiting team that he was interested in moving back to the Midwest because his parents lived there. The company was impressed by Trail's engineering experience, but they didn't offer him a job on the spot.

Recalled Sheila Hayter, director of employee services at Ferrellgas, "He was real eager to come and work for us and he kept calling to follow up that first meeting."

It wasn't long before the firm offered Trail a post as a

district manager working out of Inver Grave Heights. He was hired in October, 1996, and was due to start the job that November.

Back in San Diego, Trail broke the news of his intended move to his friends, including Andrew Cunanan. Cunanan was visibly shocked. Trail seemed to have little idea of the impact he had had on Cunanan.

"Andrew was heartbroken. Jeff had become an icon in his life even though they didn't have a relationship going," explained one friend from the Hillcrest district of San Diego.

But Trail took little notice of what his friends were saying about how heartbroken Cunanan was. He had already lined up an apartment in Bloomington and a new lover from San Diego had agreed to travel to the Midwest with him.

But Trail did promise to keep in touch with Cunanan and even insisted that Cunanan come up and visit him in Bloomington whenever he wanted. Cunanan fully intended to take up the offer sooner rather than later.

Throughout this period, Cunanan continued to service a number of older gay men on the Hillcrest circuit. Not only did they pay him discretely, but he even managed to persuade one man to give him a brand-new credit card in exchange for sex on demand. That gave him the perfect means to pay for a trip to see Jeffrey Trail when the time was right.

In January of 1997, Andrew Cunanan became very worried by a series of minor illnesses that seemed impossible to shake off.

He went for a series of medical checkups—including an AIDS test—at a local hospital.

A few weeks later, Cunanan went for medical advice to a nonprofit organization called David's Place, in San Diego. He met a counselor called Mike Dudley and got straight to the point.

"I want to know how you get AIDS and what the chances are that I've got it," Cunanan asked Dudley.

Then Cunanan reeled off a list of all the sex acts he'd been involved in. He was extremely explicit about what he'd done. And in some ways very proud.

"Many of those acts are a sort of gray area," replied Dudley, who was gaining the clear impression that Cunanan was trying to pluck up the courage to tell him he was infected.

Dudley then asked Cunanan outright if he was HIV-positive.

Cunanan exploded with fury, got up, and kicked the wall before turning to Dudley.

"If I find out who did this to me, I'm gonna get them," he screamed.

The startled counselor then tried to sooth Cunanan's out-of-control emotions. "Come on, honey, calm down. You can't think that way about anyone," Dudley told Cunanan.

Dudley gave Cunanan a hug and a squeeze and asked him if he was OK.

"Yes, I'm OK," came Cunanan's response.

The encounter was brief but indelible. Mike Dudley was left with the clear impression that Andrew Cunanan was HIV-positive.

All his friends observed that this moment was the biggest turning point in Andrew Cunanan's life. Whatever the state of his health, Cunanan decided there and then that he was going to do what the hell he wanted with anyone he could find. His bitterness was imploding.

He didn't care about being responsible. Why should he care? He didn't owe anyone anything, and he was angry that someone along the way had infected him without even bothering to warn him they had AIDS.

He had a long list of suspects but first of all he wanted to go and see his great friend Jeff Trail in Minneapolis. At least he couldn't be guilty of infecting him.

So when Cunanan heard that Trail and his new lover had

split up after just a few weeks together he immediately activated his plans.

Cunanan's stay in Trail's apartment in the Minneapolis suburb of Bloomington turned into a constant round of partying and lavish meals at some of the city's finest restaurants, most of which were paid by Cunanan on his credit card.

During one meal, Cunanan bumped into former boyfriend David Madson, whom he had briefly had a relationship with in San Francisco some years previously. Madson had split from Cunanan because he refused to give him a phone number or address where he lived, and Madson was highly suspicious about how Cunanan made a living.

But in Minneapolis all those doubts were forgotten as Madson and Cunanan revived their friendship. In the back of his mind, Cunanan wondered if Madson had infected him, although there were many other more likely suspects.

Jeff Trail was impressed by handsome Madson and the threesome became a firm fixture on the Minneapolis gay scene throughout Cunanan's five-week stay in the Midwest.

Cunanan never once revealed whether or not he'd just discovered he was HIV-positive.

David Madson—whose family lived in the Midwest—had a background very similar to Jeff Trail's. He came from a religious, happy, outdoor family. It was almost as if Andrew Cunanan were trying to reassure himself that it was possible to be gay and come from a secure background. He certainly hadn't any such reassurances from his own upbringing.

Madson was born in 1963, in Waterloo, Iowa, the youngest of four children.

In his early childhood years, the family moved on to the Wisconsin cities of Reedsburg, Madison, Wausau, and Appleton, before they settled in Barron in 1978 when Madson was fourteen.

Madson fitted in well in the small town, although being the son of the owners of a prominent downtown business, a Coast to Coast hardware store, certainly made the adjustment even easier.

At high school, Madson participated in baseball and golf, and was a top competitor in forensics. He played in the band, made the honor roll, and served on the student council. He was a Boy Scout and a member of the National Honor Society. He won the state Quiz Bowl in 1981 and 1982 and nine medals in statewide debating competition. He played varsity baseball and varsity golf.

The family reveled in their summer outings at their Island Lake, Wisconsin, cabin where David became an excellent water-skier. He was so particular about things that he drew a map of the lake to show his dad where he wanted the motorboat driven.

He also played the lead role of Professor Harold Hill in the school's production of *The Music Man*.

Madson eventually graduated from the University of Minnesota in Minneapolis with a master's degree in architectural design and engineering. During that period he worked as a ski instructor. He also developed and published an urban development plan for the downtown Duluth waterfront renovation project. And he was a guest lecturer at Harvard University on architectural engineering and even designed a traveling AIDS memorial.

After college, Madson initially worked as an investigator for law firms, and for Saks Fifth Avenue department store in Minneapolis.

By the time he met up with Cunanan and Trail, Madson was a snappy dresser, kept himself in top physical shape, and worked long hours as a valued retail space designer for John Ryan and Co., in Minneapolis. He was also devoted to his dalmatian dog Prints and famous for his one-arm hugs.

Madson was steadfastly loyal to his friends and encour-

aged all around him to do their best. He was noted as someone who was always prepared to listen. His two sisters were
both married and he had several nieces and nephews.

Madson religiously sent Christmas and birthday cards to
friends and family. He never forgot Mother's or Father's Day
and he even remembered his parent's wedding anniversary
every year.

Madson was also always prepared to help those more
needy than himself and would regularly buy groceries for
older people in the apartment block where he lived. He also
delivered baskets of treats at Easter, Thanksgiving, and
Christmas. He even made special Christmas ornaments for
his nieces and nephews.

At dinners in restaurants, Madson's laughter was so infec-
tious that people at other tables smiled. He nearly always
managed to make whoever he was talking to feel as if they
were the most important person in the world.

When a college friend was feeling blue over a dating dry
spell, Madson showed up at her door with a tuxedo, top hat,
and cane and took her out for a night of dinner and dancing.

And when Madson heard that Cunanan's friend Jeff Trail
had not managed to make many friends since moving to Minneapolis the previous fall, he tried to help him. It was typical
of Madson.

His oldest friend Rich Bonnin explained, "David felt sorry
for Trail. The guy had moved here with a partner, with a
boyfriend. They broke up shortly after he got here. He didn't
know many people, didn't have that many friends at first."

Madson's hobbies by the time he reconnected with Andrew Cunanan were music, cooking, and a nonstop addiction
to building things.

As his sister Diane Benning would later recall, "He was
as clean as a whistle—no drugs, no smoking, no guns. You
couldn't get a cleaner-cut kid."

Madson had only one major downnote in an otherwise stellar life.

That had occurred several years earlier, during an acrimonious breakup of a two-year relationship with another lover, which led to Madson obtaining a court no-contact order that the man violated. That same man later claimed that Madson was not so perfect and even said he was not beyond violence.

On an everyday note, Madson was proud of how he meticulously planned his finances down to the last penny.

When David Madson recalled all this to Cunanan after they had reconnected, Cunanan felt even more attracted to him because he seemed to represent the personification of what he aspired to be. But he also felt jealous of David Madson and Jeff Trail because they both seemed to have a much better life than him.

Cunanan was envious that Madson and Trail's families appeared to have accepted their sexuality. He sorely wished the same could have been said for himself.

Eight

THE FAME GAME

In Minneapolis, David Madson showed Cunanan and Jeff Trail around the urban-artsy neighborhood where he lived. Madson dressed well and liked to dance. He ate out often at upscale restaurants such as the Monte Carlo Bar and cafe and hip places across the river such a Nye's Polonaise Room. Madson also made a point of lifting weights at the nearby Arena Health Club most evenings before going out on the town.

And Cunanan insisted on paying for all the meals and entertainment.

Once, at dinner in a typically expensive Minneapolis restaurant, the maitre d' brought a wine list, only to be waved away by Cunanan who announced grandly: "Just bring me the most expensive bottle you have."

One of the guests that night called Madson the next morning, and Madson asked the man what he thought of Cunanan.

"I didn't care for him, he was very showy and flashy," came the swift reply. "I'd watch out for him. He's trouble."

At another party in Minneapolis, Cunanan and Madson met *Friends* actress Lisa Kudrow and Cunanan cornered her about his so-called attempts to become an actor and even managed to get her to agree to pose in a photo taken by his friend David Madson.

Writer Todd Raines, a fellow guest, later recalled: "Cunanan had been boring us all about having Hollywood contacts and how he felt he was going to make it in the movie business.

"Within seconds he was sitting next to Lisa like a limpet, despite being told not to bother her. He wouldn't leave her side all night.

"You could see she was desperate. She kept looking around as if for help, and he kept tapping on her shoulder to get her attention.

"The more she tried to get away the more irritated and persistent he became. After about an hour she just got up and walked away saying she was going to the bathroom, and never went back. His face was like thunder.

"He tried to put a brave front on it, but you could tell he was furious with her."

However Cunanan thoroughly enjoyed his stay in the Midwest although it left him with a very difficult dilemma. He was extremely attracted to both Jeff Trail and David Madson. He actually told one friend he didn't know which one he preferred.

In the end he went back to San Diego—because it was a far easier option than staying in Minneapolis and getting even more eaten up with jealousy. But for Cunanan it was an extremely close-fought decision.

"I'm going to go back to San Diego and reality," Cunanan told one friend. "I've got to make a living, you know."

Cunanan undoubtedly preferred to escape such dilemmas rather than face them head-on. It was just like his AIDS "problem," which was burning inside him but he didn't want to face up to it by telling any of his friends.

En route to San Diego, Cunanan decided to visit some friends in Los Angeles.

But on arrival in West Hollywood he discovered that most

of the people whose numbers and addresses he'd gathered over the previous couple of years were not interested in seeing him.

So he went looking for some new friends.

One night on West Hollywood's infamous gay strip at Santa Monica Boulevard, Cunanan picked up a man named Tim Schwager at a bar.

The two hit it off immediately and Schwager agreed to go to a nearby hotel with Cunanan.

Settling into a room they continued talking and ordered beers and chicken noodle soup. Suddenly the room began swimming and Schwager realized his drink had been spiked with drugs.

He collapsed on the bed and came round to find Cunanan looming over him reaching for his throat.

"At that moment he had murder in his heart—I could see it in his eyes," Schwager later recalled.

Summoning all his energy, Schwager, who regularly worked out, flailed his fists and managed to threw Cunanan off him.

But then he passed out again and awoke to find himself naked.

Schwager continued: "I shudder to think of it now because he could quite easily have killed me at any time during the hours I was drugged and unconscious.

"I always thought I'd know if someone was dangerous, but I didn't. Cunanan was unappealing physically and a little odd, but until that moment I woke with him sitting over me he looked like any other ordinary guy in the street."

Schwager left the hotel in a hurry. He never forgot the smile on Andrew Cunanan's face as he lay on the bed looking like a satisfied cat who'd just got the cream.

* * *

During that same trip to Hollywood, Cunanan—now drinking quite heavily for the first time in his life—turned up at a show business reception where he met a number of famous names, including British actress Liz Hurley—live-in lover of Hugh Grant—and renowned for wearing revealing dresses designed by Gianni Versace.

Cunanan told one friend he adored Hurley because she was such a "movie star vamp."

Like a lot of gay men he liked glitzy over-the-top stars like Hurley. In some ways they represented their dreams come true. They considered them classy.

But Hurley completely ignored Cunanan when he tried to strike up a conversation with her.

Later, Cunanan told a friend: "She's a bitch from hell. Who the fuck does she think she is?"

Then Cunanan added with even more bitchy venom in his voice: "I thought she had a lot of nerve being like that after her boyfriend went off with that prostitute. Who does she think she is?"

Cunanan told one friend that he didn't like Hugh Grant because he'd tried out as an extra on Grant's movie *Nine Months* but wasn't hired. Cunanan was growing into a more and more vindictive character.

But Cunanan proudly told anyone who'd listen that he also met a host of other celebrities including Madonna.

"What was she like? Tell me. Tell me," said one friend anxiously.

"Well, physically she's kinda cute, but I didn't like her attitude toward me. She treated me like I was nothing."

There was a certain tone of resentment in Cunanan's voice. And it was going to build and build within him. He had the virus and he wished some of them did as well.

While in Hollywood, Cunanan found himself short of money, so he turned to the only way he knew to escape financial problems.

Angelyne is a Jayne Mansfield lookalike who first took out a billboard in Hollywood in the late eighties, advertising herself as an actress. "Call Angelyne" is the admonition. There is no evidence she ever had a major role. However, she has achieved fame as a traffic hazard in Hollywood, thanks to numerous posters featuring her in pink and gold lame, rumored to have been paid for by her rich Arab lover.

A vast fifty-foot by twenty-five-foot Angelyne billboard looked down on the corner of Santa Monica Boulevard and La Brea Avenue where Andrew Cunanan was standing dressed in a figure-hugging dress, tights and high stiletto heels. It was 2.30 A.M. Yet to some passersby he was just about as appealing as Angelyne.

Desperate times called for desperate measures and Cunanan was trying to make some fast bucks to help extend his stay in Los Angeles. Over five consecutive nights in the early spring of 1997, he worked as a transvestite prostitute.

Later, he told one San Diego friend that he picked up more than a dozen men and had full sex with a number of them while performing indecent acts with others.

"One of them looked real familiar. I think he was that old guy who plays the grandpa on that TV show," Cunanan boasted about one customer.

He also claimed that one giant Hollywood star pulled his four-wheel drive truck alongside him and was about to cut a deal when an LAPD black-and-white appeared on the horizon. The star drove off with a screech of tires.

It was a measure of just how far Cunanan would go to survive that he was quite prepared to sell himself on a street corner dressed in drag if that meant he could do what the hell he wanted.

Eventually, Cunanan returned to the more familiar surroundings of the Hillcrest district of San Diego. He was feeling increasingly stressed by his HIV predicament and had become obsessed by trying to work out who might have given him the disease.

But none of this stopped Cunanan from trying to find himself yet another older partner. He even admitted to his closest friends that he no longer enjoyed the company of older men, but he had little choice if he were going to survive.

Virtually none of his friends knew whether he was HIV positive.

Around this time, Cunanan moved into a small studio apartment and sold his car.

His roommate at the new apartment, platonic friend Erik Greenman, got quite a shock when he walked into Cunanan's bedroom one morning to find that he had turned his room into a shrine to Hollywood star Tom Cruise. The walls were covered in newspaper clippings and posters of the actor.

Cunanan smiled and explained: "I want to tie Cruise up, use him, and make him beg for more. I love him."

Greenman politely coughed and was about to leave the room when Cunanan told him he hated Cruise's wife Nicole Kidman because she was married to his idol.

"I'd like to kill her so I can have Tom to myself," he told Greenman.

Greenman decided not to take Cunanan seriously. Lots of gay men got turned on by Cruise despite the star's own well-publicized heterosexuality.

In fact Cunanan often rented five Tom Cruise videos at a time and watched them all in one evening at the apartment. Sometimes he'd even study them virtually frame by frame, watching every one of the actor's gestures.

One day Cunanan told Greenman: "Tom ages like fine wine. He's the perfect boy toy."

Cruise actually represented everything that Andrew Cunanan wanted in a partner—hairless, boyish face with an incredible frame.

"That's my dream lover," Cunanan boasted to Greenman.

Not long after moving into the apartment, Cunanan's roommate walked in unexpectedly early from work to find Cunanan watching a hard core gay porn video.

"Hey, Erik, look at what I'd like to do to Tom Cruise."

The video featured a young man strapped to a chair while being tortured with an electric cattle prod.

"I want to tie Cruise up, use him, and make him beg for more."

That night Cunanan announced he was going out to a local gay bar.

"You could say I'm Tom Cruising!" Cunanan joked as he walked out of the door.

On March 8 and 9, 1997, Cunanan had two heavy nights out in one of the most notorious gay bars in Hillcrest.

Cunanan was in a wild, reckless party mood on both occasions and even persuaded a male porn star to pose with him for photos taken by a man Cunanan had picked up just a few minutes earlier.

That man later recalled: "He seemed like just another guy out for a good time when I saw him. He wanted me to take his picture and was spending money like there was no tomorrow."

The photo clearly showed that Cuanan had put on at least thirty pounds in the previous few months and he seemed very distracted.

But then he had a lot on his mind.

Friends and associates in San Diego noticed that around this time, Cunanan stopped working out in the gym and started adding vodka to his cranberry juice for the first time in living memory. His hair, once so carefully molded, was often unkempt.

Unbeknownst to many, Cunanan also began selling pain killers as a way to make some extra money.

Cunanan had become a gigolo without a gig and the phone had fallen silent.

His once trim and muscled frame began to bloat. He'd long since been cut off from his monthly allowances and luxury cars.

As one of his friends later explained: "For someone driven by maniacal ego, this was a crushing blow.

"You have to understand the environment in that elite group—getting into your late twenties was getting old."

There was a combination of facts in Cunanan's life making him very depressed: his belief he was HIV positive. His looks had left him. His inner confidence and self-esteem were crumbling.

Cunanan's one-time regular workouts had been replaced by some of the downer drugs he was trying to sell.

Though he had frequently worn glasses, Cunanan began appearing virtually all the time in contact lenses, a change that so altered his look and image that many did not recognize him when he hung out in his old Hillcrest haunts.

He had completely dropped his preppy appearance and replaced it with plain jeans and T-shirt and closely cropped hair.

On a brief visit to see friends in San Francisco in mid-April, 1997, Cunanan walked into one his favorite hangouts.

Jesse Cappachionse, manager of the Midnight Star bar in the Castro district recalled, "He seemed a little more subdued. Before he'd always been a little loud and boisterous. But this time around he was drinking, which I thought was odd."

Throughout this period Cunanan had kept in close contact with David Madson in Minneapolis. He actually believed that perhaps they could restart their relationship. It was his only hope.

While in San Francisco, Cunanan met up with old friend Steve Gomer.

"I think I've found the perfect relationship," he told Gomer.

"That's great news," replied Gomer. "What makes this guy so special?"

Cunanan hesitated for a moment then a sly grin wiped across his face.

"He lets me do anything I want . . . and I mean anything!"

Cunanan meant sexually: the conversation then turned to discussions of sex toys such as latex masks used for bondage. That equated to love in the eyes of Andrew Cunanan.

"The ones with the noses and the mouths cut out?" asked Steve Gomer.

"Just the noses," answered Cunanan.

During that same trip to San Francisco, Cunanan met up with another old friend called Philip Horne, a twenty-nine-year-old civil rights lawyer. Cunanan told Horne he'd found a two-bedroom apartment in the Marina district of the city and intended to move there.

"He was looking for a roommate and I was looking for an apartment at the time, so it was a perfect arrangement," Horne later recalled.

Cunanan promised to call Horne the next day to hammer out the final details on the apartment. But Cunanan never called Horne and headed back south to San Diego instead.

Back in Hillcrest, Cunanan tried to revive a friendship with an elderly ex-partner, who was a San Diego businessman. He needed financial support.

Cunanan began selling more and more drugs and, increasingly, consuming them. In Hillside bars, he'd moan to bartenders that he couldn't get any dates.

To barkeep Nigel Mayer at Flicks, the gay hangout in San Diego, Cunanan seemed tired and despondent.

One night in April, 1997, he told a friend about his plans

to move to San Francisco. "I'm not coming back. People don't know me. They think they do, but they don't."

Among Cunanan's friends and associates in San Diego, the word was finally spreading that he might have contracted AIDS.

Cunanan no longer had the free-flowing credit cards. Besides some money raised by drug dealing and occasionally sleeping with men for money, he was flat broke.

Cunanan also became increasingly jealous of Jeffrey Trail and David Madson, whom he believed were seeing each other in Minneapolis behind his back.

On April 20, Cunanan telephoned Jeff Trail and asked him outright if he was having a relationship with Madson. The conversation became very heated. Cunanan screamed profanities at his onetime friend. Trail tried to calm things down but to no avail. Then Cunanan's voice changed tone and he said calmly, "I'm going to kill you, Jeffrey Trail. You're dead."

Then the phone line went dead.

Later that same day Trail told one Minneapolis friend, "I've made a lot of enemies this weekend . . . I've got to get out of here. They're going to kill me."

It all sounded a little over dramatic. But Jeff Trail had a feeling that something bad might be about to happen.

Cunanan's rapid slide into depression gained even more speed that evening when he attended a dinner party at the California Cuisine restaurant, in the Hillcrest district. Cunanan ordered the finest Champagne and ate a vast dish of roast ostrich.

Toward the end of the meal, Cunanan announced he was moving to San Francisco.

"But first," said Cunanan. "I have to take care of some business in Minnesota."

He'd already bought the one-way airline ticket.

Nine

FIRST BLOOD

W hat Andrew Cunanan had not revealed to his friends at that last dinner party was that he was so broke he'd had to plead with his credit card company to advance the money for that one-way ticket to Minneapolis. He was already well over his $20,000 limit.

On arrival at Minneapolis Airport in the late afternoon of April 26, 1997, Cunanan was picked up by David Madson. The two men headed back to Madson's home in the Harmony Lofts apartment building, in the Warehouse district of the city.

Friends of Madson had warned him to be careful of Cunanan. Close friend Rich Bonnin had even telephoned Madson that Friday afternoon and was surprised when Madson told him he was planning to pick up Cunanan at the Minneapolis-St.Paul International Airport and let him stay at his apartment for the weekend.

Bonnin quizzed Madson, who'd earlier said he intended to cut off contact with Cunanan. Madson even admitted he had visited Cunanan briefly in San Diego over the previous Easter weekend.

"I thought you weren't going to have anything to do with this guy," Bonnin asked Madson. "Why are you letting him stay with you?"

"Well, I think he needs a friend and I think he's trying to get his life straightened out. He just needs somebody," Madson assured his friend.

It was a typical statement of Madson. He was always willing to help troubled individuals.

On the first night of Cunanan's stay in Minneapolis, he and Madson went out with some of Madson's friends, whom Cunanan annoyed by bragging loudly about driving a Rolls Royce convertible.

Apart from that it was a very quiet, normal evening.

At nine the following evening, Jeff Trail told his own current live-in lover Jon Hacket that Cunanan was in town staying at Madson's apartment and he was going to meet them at a coffee shop.

Hacket was surprised because Trail had admitted a few days earlier that he had had a huge falling out with Cunanan during that phone conversation.

But that night Trail assured Hacket everything was cool between him and Cunanan and he'd meet up with Hacket later that night at the Gay 90s, a popular Minneapolis gay club.

But at Madson's apartment, Trail and Cunanan began arguing once again. Trail wanted Cunanan to get himself sorted out. Neither Madson or Trail realized their friend believed he was HIV-positive. They felt he was under immense pressure for some reason they could not work out.

As Cunanan and Trail argued with increasing ferocity, Madson apparently stood by without doing anything.

About ten P.M. one of David Madson's neighbors heard the loud argument coming from Madson's apartment. Someone was shouting "Get the fuck out!" and the wall was shaking. More shouting followed and a series of thuds that lasted for thirty to forty seconds, then there was a cold beat of silence.

In fact Andrew Cunanan had grabbed a claw hammer from the kitchen, walked back into the living room, and bludgeoned Jeff Trail at least fifteen times with it until he collapsed on the floor

Then he bent over Trail's bloodied body and crashed the hammer into him at least another ten times until Trail no longer moved. His blood had splattered the walls and ceilings and Cunanan was soaked in it as well.

Trail's watch stopped at 9:55 on April 27, 1997, in the middle of the murder frenzy.

Neighbor Jesse Shadoan later recalled: ''It was kinda scary, but when the noises stopped I guessed there was nothing to worry about.''

The silence was eventually broken by the sound of running water inside Madson's apartment.

Cunanan and David Madson tried to clear the red stains off the walls and floor near the body. Madson was so nervous that he managed to smear the blood over an even wider area. It was in the rugs, the floorboards, everywhere.

Then Cunanan pulled an Oriental rug out of the bedroom and rolled Jeff Trail's blood-covered body up in it. He told Madson that when the time was right they would have to dump the body somewhere it could never be found.

For the following few days Madson and Cunanan carried on living in the spacious loft apartment as if nothing much had happened, even though Jeff Trail's rotting corpse was just a few feet from them.

Witnesses even saw Cunanan and Madson walking Madson's dog in the streets near his apartment block. They looked like a happy couple.

On April 29, after Madson's coworkers grew concerned because he had failed to show up for work, they contacted the caretaker of his apartment building.

The caretaker, accompanied by a neighbor, entered Madson's apartment with a passkey. They immediately noticed a pool of blood on the hall floor.

Then they found Trail's body rolled up in that blood-soaked rug. They retreated and called the police.

Cunanan and Madson were actually in the apartment when they heard the caretaker enter. They hid in a bedroom. As soon as the caretaker and the neighbor left, they slipped out of a fire exit and headed for Madson's red Jeep Cherokee. In the rush to escape the apartment, David Madson had left behind his wallet and credit cards.

If the caretaker had looked closer they would have noticed that Madson's dog had just been fed.

Police rapidly found the blood-covered claw hammer near Trail's body. From the vast number of wounds they knew they were dealing with a brutal, emotion-charged murder.

On Trail's answering machine detectives found a message from Cunanan inviting Trail to Madson's apartment. Also in the apartment, not far from the hammer, police discovered a nylon gym bag containing a gun holster.

The bag had Cunanan's name on it. Also nearby was an empty Remington Peters gunbox with distinctive Golden Sabre .40 caliber bullets in it. The gun had been bought by Jeff Trail when he was training to join the California Highway Patrol.

Investigators soon deduced that the perpetrators of the crime had stolen the gun and ten lethal Golden Sabre bullets.

Jeff Trail's parents—Stanley, a retired mathematics professor who taught at the Northern Illinois University and mother Ann, a retired public elementary school teacher—were both devastated by his death.

"It sounds trite, but he was a wonderful son and we're

going to really miss him," Ann Trail told journalists the day after their son was found murdered.

"He was kind, caring. He had very few bad habits," explained Stanley Trail. "He went out of his way to be helpful to people."

Mr. Trail insisted this was not just a father's pride. "This is what I've gleaned from people."

On May 2, 1997, David Madson's red Jeep with a Vail ski area bumper sticker was spotted heading north out of Minneapolis on Interstate 35.

Shortly after one P.M. Madson and Cunanan, dressed in khaki shorts and open shirts, walked into the Full Moon bar and restaurant in a speck of a town called Stark, just off the highway.

Cunanan requested a seat out on the deck despite the gray, blustery weather that day. He ordered two Grainbelt beers and a California cheeseburger basket.

"I'll have the same," muttered David Madson to owner Jean Rosen as she took their order.

She noticed that Madson kept looking over his shoulder every time the front door to the bar opened. But he showed absolutely no fear of his companion.

They sat across from each other at a picnic table and talked earnestly, sometimes smiling, sometimes touching hands, all through lunch.

After the meal, Cunanan drove Madson further north on I-35 towards Duluth. Suddenly, without explanation, he pulled off the road onto a track that led to an abandoned farmhouse next to East Rush Lake, about forty-five miles north of Minneapolis, in Chicago County.

Then Cunanan pulled out Jeff Trail's Golden Saber .40 caliber pistol and ordered David Madson out of the vehicle.

He considered the first shot, aimed and fired. Madson's body jerked. He cocked the hammer on the heavy weapon with his thumb and fired another right behind the first. Madson was down on his hands, trying to get up. He clawed at Cunanan's legs with his hands.

Cunanan stepped closer, centered the five-and-half-inch barrel at Madson's eye. Cocked and fired. Madson's head jumped. Cunanan heard him make these noises, little grunts and moans. He stood over him as his knees gave way immediately and he slumped into the foot-long grass. He made no more noises.

The brilliant pool of light bathing the scene heightened the blue and purple lividity staining David Madson's broad, sagging face. A pair of sunglasses lay askew across his forehead. The short-sleeved shirt gave way to heavy bloodstains across the upper torso.

Chicago County Sheriff Randall Schwegman carefully stepped to his right and noted the entry wounds in the head. The victim's light-colored shorts had clear grass stains on the thighs and crotch as though he had been rolling around. On his left wrist he still wore a watch. On the left, a gold band.

Then the sheriff noticed the ants. A flurry of them. All over the body. Schwegman's eyes traveled back to the pants and the shirt. They looked expensive, made by some fancy designer no doubt, he thought.

The assistant county medical examiner came up behind Schwegman as the investigator hunkered down alongside the victim.

"I'd say it's second-stage rigor mortis, Randall. Sixteen to eighteen hours. Just like this."

Although the floodlights from the evidence unit were more than enough for good exposure, the police technician's 35mm camera went off with a flash each time he snapped its shutter, methodically documenting every inch of the body and its surroundings.

Schwegman—a solid heavyweight with a bulldog jaw somewhat softened by a set of aviator-style glasses—stepped out of the whiteness and waited until the technician had finished up. Then he and a deputy continued examining the body of David Madson, which had been discovered a few hours earlier on that hot May 3 day by two fishermen about to cast their rods on East Rush lake.

They'd found David Madson's corpse lying on its back near some tire tracks in the grass. Close to the body were three bullet casings from that .40 caliber gun.

"He knew it was coming," Schwegman told his deputy as they turned the corpse. "He knew he was going to get it. Look at those defensive wounds on his fingers."

Now Andrew Cunanan had seven bullets left.

Madson's family immediately insisted that Madson could not have been involved in the murder of Jeff Trail, despite police claims to the contrary.

"There is no way possible. It's totally inconceivable, totally out of character to think that," said Madson's father, Howard, shortly after his son's body was found.

Madson's sister, Nancy Young, of Portage, Michigan, recalled her brother's first and only hunting trip, when he was ten. After his father shot a duck, David cried so hard and became so traumatized that he never hunted again. That epitomized his lifelong loathing of violence of any sort.

Howard and Carol Madson—David's mother—remain convinced to this day that their son walked in on Trail's murder and thus became Cunanan's hostage for the next five days. Finally, they believe Madson may have tried to escape Cunanan only to be shot.

"First and foremost, he was a bright, enthusiastic, very talented designer . . . He would have been one of the leading designers in the world," said his employer John Ryan, in Minneapolis shortly after Madson's murder.

"Additionally, he was extremely responsible, reliable and detail-orientated . . . You don't always get those all wrapped up in a creative, talented person. He's left a big hole and we will certainly miss him."

And the most baffling aspect to the family was how Madson could allow himself to get caught up with a character like Cunanan.

His father Howard explained: "Two friends told me he was worried about Cunanan. Why didn't he follow his better judgement is a question we'll never know the answer to."

Following Madson's murder, both his mother and father were touched by the outpouring of support they received, as well as the hundreds of written or spoken tributes to their son. They even set up a scholarship fund in his name.

They also remained secure in their Christian faith. "We know where he stands. We know where he is today," said Howard Madson. "The good Lord had him in his arms before he hit the ground."

Sheriff Randy Schwegman of Chicago County headed down to San Diego to search Cunanan's apartment within days of the discovery of Madson's body.

The first thing that struck him as strange was the shrine to Tom Cruise.

Then he found a trove of S&M gear; clamps, harnesses, and videos featuring brutal sex with animals, some of them with titles like "Target for Torture" and "Pushed to the Limit".

Schwegman immediately noticed Cunanan's bed was made, which suggested he intended to return.

There was a bizarre red stain on the bedroom wall, a glass on the night table, a hairbrush from the bathroom drawer, a bottle of cologne and its box, bills from the kitchen trash can, charred paper from the fireplace, a memo book, and several letters, including one from Madson. It didn't look as though he'd departed forever.

Schwegman also located three photos of Cunanan, one of which would be used in the wanted poster that was to be issued immediately.

The collection of photos from Cunanan's apartment showed the suspect in a range of expressions and hairstyles.

Schwegman also found Cunanan's 1997 diary as they searched the premises. In it they discovered an entry that clearly implied where Cunanan was heading after the murders of Jeff Trail and David Madson.

Cunanan had written: "If I need to get lost, it's going to be New York."

Then Schwegman searched a pile of laundry in the bedroom. He later noted: "I'm not into fashion, but I knew these were good clothes. I didn't pay any attention to the labels."

If he had looked closer he would have seen that many of the clothes were made by Versace.

After talking to Cunanan's roommate, Schwegman decided that he'd better alert authorities in California that Tom Cruise should take some extra security precautions.

With Madson and Trail dead, and Cunanan missing, Minnesota authorities immediately notified local and federal authorities for help. They even stretched the truth about the amount of evidence against the suspect in order to get a federal fugitive warrant issued.

Investigators were frustrated by finding themselves chasing a suspect with no criminal history and no past indications of violent behavior.

San Diego police watched Cunanan's modest apartment in Hillcrest in case he returned. Police were using standard procedure for capturing murder suspects, the majority of which usually got panicky and ran home to hide, even though it was the first place the police would look.

But Cunanan did not return to San Diego.

Even with the two dead, police were convinced they would wrap the case up quickly.

"I figured he'd get caught in a few days or maybe go off and kill himself," explained San Diego Police Lieutenant Jim Collins.

Instead, Andrew Cunanan's trail went dead.

Ten

CASUALTY OF WAR

Lee Miglin, seventy-two, was a high-powered, hard-chasing Chicago builder, a guy who made a bundle in the real estate business during the go-go eighties boom, but somehow he never fit the stereotype.

Lee Miglin grew up in downtown Danville, Illinois, son of a coal miner from Lithuania. Business was in his blood from the start. As a young man he paid for a trip from California to Chicago by selling sunglasses and pancake mix at gas stations as he made his way east.

Miglin was a classic American success story. He would eventually be credited with inventing the business park—developments that combined office and warehouse space.

Miglin and his partner, J. Paul Beitler, built several skyscrapers and created millions of square feet of office space, but they were best known for a project that never happened.

It was going to be the world's tallest building—a slender, sleek 125-story tower called the "Sky Needle"—and it got a lot of publicity in 1989, chiefly because Beitler promoted it heavily. Miglin, characteristically, preferred to stay in the background, working on the financing. But when the building boom went bust the following year, the project faded away.

Stanley Tigerman, an architect who worked for Miglin on the creation of the Chicago Bar Association Building, later explained: "Lee was not the typical real estate developer. He was a terrific, gentle, sweet guy. Very self-effacing. He was never the type to blow his own horn."

"He was definitely not anything like Donald Trump," said Mark Jerasek, who worked with Miglin for twelve years. "He was a gentleman in the truest sense of the word."

Miglin remained a major figure in Chicago business circles. Just as driven was his wife Marilyn Miglin, the Chicago nightclub chorus girl Lee married thirty-eight years earlier.

She became a successful businesswoman, owner of a cosmetics and perfume company and a popular Chicago makeup salon. As flamboyant as her husband was shy, Marilyn, fifty-nine, pitched her Destiny and Magic perfumes on TV's Home Shopping Network. It worked: Her company, Marilyn Miglin L.P., reported sales of more than $25 million in 1994, earning her the nickname "the Queen of Makeovers."

Explained Stanley Tigerman, "He was very proud of her and very much in love with her. He always talked about her."

Together, the Miglins were active in Chicago's social and charity scenes, raising money for the University of Chicago Hospitals and the Museum of Science and Industry, among other causes.

The couple, who had two grown children, lived in an elegantly renovated home in the upmarket Chicago lakefront neighborhood known as the Gold Coast.

The wrought-iron fences and stately brick townhouses that make up the Gold Coast rarely saw any crimes. The only people out on the streets tended to be those walking dogs such as shar-pei puppies and immaculately groomed Lhasa apsos. The cars parked in garages and on the streets were Jaguars and Range Rovers.

The Miglins' home on East Scott Street was actually two row houses, one red-bricked and one brown, combined several years earlier so Lee and Marilyn would have an expansive kitchen, overlooking their backyard garden and pond. Inside the house, the dominant color was cream; on the walls the Miglins hung Renoirs and Monets.

The house perfectly reflected the Miglins' ascent to the pinnacles of their respective professions.

Marilyn Miglin spoke to her husband at two P.M. on May 3 from Toronto where she was promoting her cosmetics on a home shopping network. She told him she intended to return next day, Sunday, and he promised to pick her up from the airport. That afternoon a neighbor saw Lee Miglin in front of the house.

Nearby, Andrew Cunanan awoke from a few hours' sleep in David Madson's red Jeep. He'd been drinking at a handful of gay bars and clubs in Chicago until he'd virtually run out of cash. Then he'd pulled the car up in a good neighborhood to take a break.

Why Lee Miglin allowed Andrew Cunanan to walk into his house will probably never be known. But it was an invitation to die.

Perhaps they'd met in a bar and struck up a friendship? Did Cunanan see Miglin in his gleaming Lexus and decide that he wanted to steal it?

Whatever the motive, within a short time of entering Lee Miglin's house, Cunanan was staging a gruesome real-life reenactment of a scene from one of his favorite gay S&M pornographic videos called "Target for Torture."

He forced Miglin into the garage of the house and bound his entire face in masking tape, cutting a hole for Miglin's nose with a sharp knife.

As Miglin stood shaking with fear, Cunanan crashed his fist over and over into Miglin's ribs and watched him fall to the ground.

Then Cunanan got out a screwdriver and pressed it hard

against Miglin's chest. The old man screamed as Cunanan then forced the screwdriver right into his chest. Then he did it again and again until Miglin passed out.

Cunanan then grabbed a garden bow saw, ignored Miglin's screams and began sawing through Miglin's throat. The blood spurted in all directions.

Throughout all this, Cunanan felt a strange sensation running through his body. He was enjoying inflicting the torture. It was a release for him. He was getting his own back for all that past suffering.

Cunanan then lay Lee Miglin's bloodied body on the garage floor in front of the property developer's green Lexus. He got in the driver's seat, started it up and drove the vehicle backwards and forwards over the body at least five times.

Then Cunanan got out, found some plastic wrapping in the corner of the garage and wrapped Miglin's entire body to stop the blood flowing out of his corpse.

His pushed the body under another car next to the Lexus and walked back into the house.

Cunanan then made himself comfortable in the Miglins' home. He made a ham sandwich and drank some orange juice from the icebox.

Then he went up to the Miglins' bedroom, made himself comfortable, watched some late-night TV, and fell asleep in their bed.

Next morning Cunanan showered, shaved, and took one of Miglin's leather jackets plus a fancy wristwatch that caught his eye the previous evening. He also pocketed ten gold coins that Miglin kept on hand to reward good employees plus $2,000 in cash he found in a briefcase belonging to Miglin.

Cunanan then headed off in Lee Miglin's Lexus for his next port of call.

He hadn't wasted any bullets this time. He knew he'd need them later.

When Marilyn Miglin arrived home on Sunday, May 4 following her out-of-town trip in Toronto she was perplexed that her husband hadn't met her at the airport.

She found the house unoccupied, the gate unlocked, whiskers in the sink, and dirty dishes and a half-eaten sandwich in the kitchen. It surprised her because Lee Miglin had always been an immaculately tidy man. Then she found what looked like a gun (it later turned out to be a fake weapon) in the couple's bathroom. She called the police.

Police who later found Lee Miglin's body in the garage noted that there were no signs of forced entry in the house. They surmised that Miglin must have known his killer. But that didn't really make it any easier to understand.

As Miglin's elderly mother later told the *Chicago Tribune*, "He died a worse death than Christ."

Meanwhile, homicide detectives concluded that the killer had deliberately left a calling card—the half-eaten ham sandwich and the whiskers in the sink.

Investigators did not publicize the fact that Miglin's body had been run over at least five times by his own Lexus and that his face had virtually been cut off by his killer.

Following the murder, Chicago Mayor Richard M. Daley praised Lee Miglin as "a tireless contributor to Chicago's charitable and cultural communities."

It wasn't until three days after the killing that Chicago police noticed David Madson's red Cherokee less than a block from the crime scene, accruing parking tickets. They called in its licence number and learned its gory history.

Andrew Cunanan immediately became the number-one suspect in the murder of Lee Miglin.

The Jeep was another taunt, a dare, a "signature" from the killer. Inside the vehicle police even found photographs of Andrew Cunanan.

There was also a map from a local Chicago tourist magazine available in hotel lobbies. A red line was marked from the north end of Chicago's Loop to a neighborhood with many gay bars.

"Why did he do that?" Minneapolis Police Sergeant Bob Ticich later asked. "He's not stupid. He speaks five languages fluently. He has a photographic memory and is well educated in the arts. He wants people to know!"

To confuse matters further, Miglin's son Duke was an actor in Los Angeles and there was a claim (never substantiated) that he was an acquaintance of Cunanan and that Cunanan had called at the Miglins' Chicago home after being told to say hello to them by Duke Miglin.

With three dead and FBI involvement in the case increasing, San Diego police searched Cunanan's home a second time, looking for dental charts that might connect him to the bite marks on victims or with the half-eaten food at Miglin's home. No dental records or name of a dentist could be found.

They also watched the S&M videos found earlier by Chicago Sheriff Randall Schwegman. One of them featured an episode in which a man was forced to wear a hood over his head with just a hole for his nose while he was whipped and beaten.

"It looked like a training film for the Miglin incident," recalled one law enforcement official.

As Andrew Cunanan headed east on the I-76 toward Philadelphia, he began using the car phone so conveniently left in the green '94 Lexus by murder victim Lee Miglin.

His intention was to travel over to I-95 and head south to Florida where he had some more unfinished business to attend to.

Cunanan actually called one of his friends in San Diego unaware that Chicago homicide detectives were tagging the car phone in the hope of working out Cunanan's location.

Investigators were delighted when he began using the phone because it meant they could pinpoint the area he was in.

Chicago police then warned their colleagues in the Philadelphia area that Cunanan was in their jurisdiction and requested that he should be apprehended immediately. The only problem was that although they knew he was in the Philadelphia area they could not work out a specific location through the car phone monitoring.

So Philadelphia police put out an APB on the Lexus and its occupant, who was said to be armed and dangerous.

Local radio stations were asked to issue an appeal to the public to be on the lookout.

In his newly acquired, immaculate green Lexus, Andrew Cunanan listened with interest to the broadcasts and immediately ripped out the cellular unit and threw it off a bridge as he sped along the freeway.

Having connected with I-95 just outside Philadelphia he decided that he needed to quickly find a good spot to abandon the car and locate a replacement vehicle.

Cunanan pulled into a tourist information booth just near the Delaware Memorial Bridge and obtained a brochure that featured points of interest, including a nearby Civil War veterans' cemetery.

Eleven

RIGHT PLACE, WRONG TIME

The wind whistled through the trees as it made its way around the somber stone markers dotted across the Finn's Point Cemetery in rural Pennsville, New Jersey. The grass and cedar spread was surrounded by marshlands, and foxtails taller than a man spread out from the walls.

The only person who greeted any mourners on this barren wasteland of death was William Reese. He had worked alone in the desolate calm for more than twenty years as the cemetery's caretaker, but the job meant much more to him than just keeping the grass trimmed and the old lodge in good repair.

When strangers arrived with an aging death certificate or some family legends, he was the one who helped them find their name on the Union or the Confederate monument. When folks bought an urn holding the ashes of a dead victim, he was the one who dug the small, discrete grave.

One of Reese's ancestors fought on the Union side in the Civil War and was buried at Finn's Point, along with a few hundred other Northerners and more than 2,300 Confederate prisoners of war who died while imprisoned in an island fort on the Delaware River.

Reese was one of the founders of the Fourteenth Brooklyn Society, a group of Civil War reenactors. He loved the history of Finn's Point. It really was his second home.

Reese had grown up in Vineland, in the heart of rural southern New Jersey and lived for years in nearby Bridgeton. He trained as an electrician but grew weary of spending the days in his car traveling from job to job. He ended up at Finn's Point.

Reese had a twelve-year-old son, Troy. His wife was a librarian at an elementary school. They all lived together peacefully in a modest clapboard house in Upper Deerfield Township, where Bill Reese planted peach and apple trees in the front yard and built an elaborate tree fort out back for his son.

The Reeses were constantly seen around town together. They traveled to Civil War reenactments. For a while they did puppet shows together, then took up another hobby, making whimsical country crafts (he built them; she painted) that they sold at fairs. They were very involved in their United Methodist Church.

Reese had been fascinated with history since high school, but recently he had cut back on the reenactments a bit. The sun was too hard on him, and he found he was less steady on his feet. In April, 1997, he confided to his friend Bob Shaw that he had MS. He wasn't complaining, he just wanted Shaw to know.

The disease might make it impossible for him to work someday, but he tried not to think about it.

On days off, Reese drove to the cemetery to raise the flag, went home, and drove back to lower it when evening came.

The place, said Shaw, a friend of thirty years, "fit him like a dress glove."

But then on May 10, 1997, a smiling stranger called Andrew Cunanan came knocking at the door of his isolated lodge in the middle of that lonely cemetery.

*　　*　　*

Bill Reese wasn't the type of person not to help a stranger in distress so when the young, dark-haired man asking directions requested a glass of water he didn't hesitate.

With Reese's radio tuned to his favorite Christian broadcasting station he invited the stranger in.

Moments later Andrew Cunanan pulled Jeff Trail's gun out of his backpack and pointed it right up close to Bill Reese's head.

Cunanan then made the bearded caretaker sit down at his desk in the tiny lodge to find the keys to his red pickup parked out back.

As soon as Bill Reese handed the keys over, Cunanan squeezed the trigger and ended the life of a man who just happened to be in the right place at the wrong time.

This time it took just one bullet. Now Cunanan had six left.

Andrew Cunanan then calmly walked outside and swapped Lee Miglin's Lexus with its Illinois plates for Bill Reese's red Chevy pickup.

He didn't even bother to remove from the Lexus a Bank of America check from his own account, one of his passports and a stack of clippings about the three previous killings, which he'd cut out of newspapers.

Later that evening, Reese's wife Rebecca arrived at the cemetery to find out what had happened to her husband. When she saw that his red Chevy pickup was missing and a green Lexus stood in its place she called the local sheriff.

Less than half an hour later police found Bill Reese's body slumped at his desk next to the radio tuned into the Christian broadcasting station.

"Bill was a man of his word," his old friend Bob Shaw later explained. "He was a humble guy too. He would take people on face value, and I think that was probably his downfall. Who looks for a crazy man to show up at a place like that?''

In Lee Miglin's Lexus, investigators also found distinctive Golden Sabre shell casings and bullet fragments that matched the three from David Madson's murder scene.

Bill Reese would have lived if Cunanan hadn't taken the Delaware Memorial Bridge Road exit off his route south on 95 from Philadelphia.

With four dead, the FBI—needing the public's assistance more than ever—finally put Cunanan on its most wanted list.

''You newspaper types laugh at that, but it helps keep it in front of the public, and that helps,'' one law enforcement officer told a reporter.

But it was going to be very difficult; for the first time since the search for Patty Hearst, the bureau had had to distribute information on the killer without his fingerprints.

The case was also taken up by the television show *America's Most Wanted*. Dozens of tips were phoned in, and Cunanan sightings were phoned in from New York to New Mexico. But the man himself continued to elude authorities.

At a national park, a ranger thought he spotted Cunanan and federal agents quickly executed a military-style raid. It turned out to be a case of mistaken identity.

As the summer of 1997 kicked in, the trail just grew colder and colder.

Hammering Bill Reese's red Chevy pickup south on I-95 on May 9, Andrew Cunanan had a lot of time to think about what he'd done. He didn't look on his crimes as evil. He was simply repaying certain people what they deserved.

Even the death of caretaker Bill Reese could be excused in his eyes because he had to swap vehicles so as to continue his mission. He tried not to think much about Reese because then he wouldn't feel too bad about what happened.

Cunanan spent two days sleeping in Reese's truck at night as he made his way south. He was surprised he attracted so little attention as he was fully aware of his wanted status from the radio he kept permanently switched on.

When he hit South Carolina he realized that he needed to either steal another car or find himself a new set of plates. He didn't much want the FBI on his tail as he still had some unfinished business to attend to.

Cunanan was in the frame of mind where he wouldn't have thought twice about killing someone if he needed something that belonged to them. So when he spotted a virtually deserted Kmart in the small township of Florence, South Carolina, he immediately pulled in and waited for the perfect moment.

It was pitch-dark in the parking lot and there were only three vehicles in the entire place. He wasn't sure whether to wait for the owner to come out or just get on with the business at hand.

Cunanan pulled up alongside another red truck similar to the one he was driving, switched his engine off and sat and waited for the coast to be clear. The truck's owner, Janet Watts, was inside doing her weekly shopping while a serial killer was in the parking lot next to her pickup.

Cunanan waited and waited. Then decided to get the plate anyway.

With Jeff Trail's lethal Remington Peters .40 pushed in his belt, he slipped out of the Chevy pickup armed with one of Bill Reese's screwdrivers, quickly unfastened the back plate—SKW 623—and slipped off into the night having achieved his mission with the minimum of attention.

A few miles further south on I-95 he pulled up once more to fix the new plate onto Bill Reese's red Chevy.

Now he felt safe to continue his drive south to Florida and his destiny.

Back at the Kmart, Janet Watts had driven off in her truck

completely unaware the plate was missing. A few days later when she realized what had happened she presumed it had fallen off while driving home.

On May 19, *Time* magazine prominently tied the killings of Reese, Miglin, Madson, and Trail together nationally for the first time.

As their reporter David Van Biema wrote:

> In isolation, the crime (the murder of Bill Reese) recalls a chilling campfire tale. But it appears to be anything but isolated. It may in fact be just one episode in a real-life horror movie, a cross-country killing spree that has triggered a nationwide manhunt. The police are looking for the man who may be driving that red pickup, a man who has been moving eastward, from San Diego to Minneapolis, Minn., to Chicago and now the New Jersey coast, using a series of stolen vehicles, a man who has been charged thus far with only one crime but about whom Philadelphia FBI spokeswoman Linda Vizi noted, "Everywhere he's been, there's been a murder."

Twelve

MIAMI VICE

Miami Beach, Florida. This is a world inhabited by drifters, loners, and pashas of petty vice. And this was where Andrew Cunanan intended to stay while he decided on his next move.

On May 10, Cunanan booked into an oceanfront room at the Normandy Plaza Hotel, on Miami Beach. He used the name close to his old San Diego alias of Andrew DeSilva with a California driver's license confirming the identity.

That false license was Cunanan's most important tool in avoiding the combined efforts of the FBI and police, which had catapulted him into the FBI Ten Most Wanted List following the murder of four innocent men.

The lobby of the Normandy Plaza was adorned with photos of celebrity guests including John Wayne, Marilyn Monroe, and Clark Gable, but it had certainly seen better days.

It had been among the first and the best examples of the deco design in Florida, all those white boxy buildings with pastel trim. But now dirty pink flamingoes adorned the facade out front.

The Normandy had opened in 1936 as a "restricted hotel"—another way of saying "whites only"—with a guest registry that included Clark Gable and Carole Lombard.

But now the clientele mainly ran to low-budget tourists and down-on-their-luck drifters.

Cunanan checked in without a suitcase, although he also had in his possession a fake French passport and an ID with one of his other aliases. Cunanan paid $35.73 a night for Room 116 for a week, cash in advance.

Hotel manager Miriam Hernandez later remembered: "He was wearing a cap and very, very dark glasses."

As Andrew Cunanan stepped through the double doors of the hotel toward his first-floor room the faint odor of urine must have hit him. The floor creaked and groaned under foot; almost louder than the bawling infants and the blare of the Zenith televisions from behind closed doors as he walked up the corridor to Room 116.

The Normandy Plaza staff soon noticed that Cunanan would often leave late at night and not return until dawn. Otherwise, he kept out of sight.

One night he visited a gay club called The Twist and picked up a local man called Gary Wilson.

Wilson danced with Cunanan for hours and then sat and drank vodka cranberry juices with him.

Wilson found Cunanan very handsome but noticed that he had a habit of never looking him directly in the eye when he talked to him.

Cunanan told Wilson he was an ex-naval officer named Andy.

After almost three hours of dancing and drinking, Cunanan asked Wilson if he wanted to go back to his hotel with him

"That's a sweet offer, but I don't think so," replied Wilson.

There was something about Cunanan that didn't add up. Wilson couldn't put his finger on it, but Cunanan seemed very edgy.

However, Cunanan mainly seemed to be biding his time. In his darkened room with its pink velvet chairs and pink-and-blue polyester bedcover, he always kept the curtain closed, never opening it to look at the ocean view.

"He was always quiet but very polite," recalled manager Miriam Hernandez. "Sometimes the guests make me feel afraid. This guy didn't."

And Cunanan never once made a phone call throughout his stay at the Normandy Plaza.

After one week at the hotel he moved up to Room 201 and started paying the weekly rate of $230.50.

"He didn't argue, he didn't get drunk, he came and went on his own," said Roger Falin, the hotel's owner. "He was like a ghost."

In those first few weeks after his arrival in Miami Beach, dinner consisted mainly of takeout subs and pizzas, but never that much. Cunanan was slowly shedding the weight he had put on in the gourmet restaurants of San Diego and the alcoholic binges that first followed his obsession with being HIV-positive.

Cunanan even kept his room so immaculate it barely needed to be cleaned.

Cunanan left his dirty towels in a bag on the doorknob so maid Georgia Escoe would not have to come in. She only cleaned his room three times throughout his stay.

"It's all right, it's clean," Cunanan would tell her over and over again.

When she did get into the room she noticed something very strange as she changed the sheets.

"I found the linens always rolled up in a tight ball. It was as if he was having a bad sleep," she said.

As Cunanan wandered the Miami Beach and South Beach districts, he became increasingly convinced that the one person in the city who might be able to help him in his predicament was Italian fashion designer Gianni Versace.

He'd bragged so much about his friendship with Versace that he was certain the designer would remember him. He also had quite a crush on one of Versace's boyfriends, whom he'd met when they encountered each other in San Francisco.

His obsession was growing by the hour.

At the Normandy Plaza, the staff continued to not pay much attention to Cunanan.

Hotel owner Roger Falin later recalled: "He came and went quietly. He left the hotel each night at around ten or eleven P.M. He must have been going out to the clubs and bars, but he didn't seem to bring anyone here. He wouldn't come back until who knows when. He was soft-spoken, nice, polite, and quiet."

Miriam Hernandez, the manager, also later recalled: "He was very gentle and nice. He had a beautiful smile and beautiful teeth."

After another week at the Normandy Plaza, Cunanan decided to pay the monthly rate, $690.50, and moved into Room 322.

He then moved Bill Reese's red pickup to a parking lot on South Beach. He wondered how long if would be before the authorities located it. He felt that its location was far enough from the Normandy Plaza to ensure he wouldn't be easily connected to the vehicle.

Every few days Cunanan wandered back to the parking lot to see how many tickets had been plastered on the windshield. It amused him that there was never any police activity by the pickup.

Cunanan had seen the occasional mention of his crimes on the TV back at his hotel and he was puzzled as to why no one had tracked down Bill Reese's vehicle.

He certainly didn't feel as if he was on the FBI's Ten Most Wanted List.

Cunanan then began dining regularly at a budget Italian restaurant next door to the Normandy Plaza, eating $2 cheese pizzas and drinking Coke.

He also shopped at a nearby Walgreen's store for grooming aids and was a regular peruser at the Pleasure Emporium, a South Beach store stocked with gay videos and sexual paraphernalia.

Clerk Jeff Walter later recalled, "He was very well-dressed, very well-spoken . . . very nice."

Cunanan then had one close escape from the authorities that he didn't even realize happened.

On June 11, almost a month after arriving in Miami Beach, a sharp-eyed worker at a restaurant spotted Cunanan.

Kenneth Benjamin, who worked at Miami Subs Grill, recognized him from the TV pictures following his first four murders.

Cunanan ordered a tuna sub. Benjamin took the order back to the kitchen and sneaked to a telephone to dial 911. Police were dispatched, but while Benjamin was still on the phone a coworker took the customer's money—$4.12, including three silver dollars—and unwittingly let him walk out the door.

When a Miami Beach police cruiser arrived five minutes later, the suspect had gone.

That restaurant was only three streets away from where Cunanan was staying at the Normandy Plaza hotel.

Increasingly aware of the nationwide TV and newspaper coverage of his crimes, Cunanan decided that he needed to be in disguise when he went out of the hotel.

His favorite reinvention was to dress as a brunette woman. He would shave his entire body of hair and put on a range of outfits he'd bought at the Whitthal Shun clothing store just near the Normandy Plaza Hotel.

Cunanan would then breeze past the sleepy hotel reception staff, safe in the knowledge that they had absolutely no idea who he was. It led the staff to later presume that Cunanan hardly ever left his room in the daytime.

In fact, he regularly cruised around South Beach in drag or wearing his trademark baseball cap and dark shades.

Cunanan knew that if he shed the weight he'd put on it could also throw off his pursuers. Cunanan went to a local gym and worked out in a desperate effort to get his body back to the condition it was in before he became convinced he was HIV-positive and began that cross-country killing spree.

At Speedo's Collins Avenue store just a short distance from the epicenter of South Beach, Cunanan bought $600 worth of clothes, including workout sweat pants, skimpy red bicycle shorts and, a classic windbreaker, and some T-shirts.

But Cunanan was becoming more and more obsessed with meeting Gianni Versace.

Some days, he would sit and watch the designer's mansion from the 11th Street Diner nearby. He'd stay in the diner for hours at a time drinking one cup of coffee and studying the area in the direction of Versace's home.

But through May and June there was no sign of the flamboyant designer.

Cunanan had read enough glossy fashion magazines to know that Versace was off some place in Europe at various fashion shows. But he continued his vigil just in case Versace slipped back into Miami for a brief visit.

At night Cunanan continued to visit some of the South Beach's most notorious gay bars. The manager of The Twist on Ocean Drive saw Cunanan at the bar on numerous occasions.

One of the club's regular celebrity customers was Gianni Versace when he was in town.

Keith Lee, who went to a Versace store party in Miami Beach in May, 1997, later recalled that his friends at the event were joking that the ''Minneapolis murderer was in town'' because of newspaper reports that wanted killer Andrew Cunanan had been seen in West Palm Beach, just ninety miles north of Miami. They had been surprised at how relaxed the security precautions were at the party.

At the Cumberland County cemetery on Sunday, June 28, they buried Cunanan's fourth victim, Bill Reese. Civil War reenactment troops gathered to pay their respects and marched to the cadence of two drummers, stopping to stand at attention at Reese's grave.

Next to his grave stood an easel with a portrait of Reese in his Civil War regalia, and a wooden cross draped with laurel and his military identification tag.

"To everything there is a season," the Reverend Paul Scull, who served as chaplain for the Thirty-fifth New Jersey Volunteers, said in the eulogy. "A tragic, senseless act took our comrade from us. His bones cry to us to carry on the message to love God and country. His heart cries, 'Be faithful to your trust.'"

Bill Reese's widow, Rebecca, stood silently next to her son, Troy. Her eyes filled with tears when her husband's identification tag was placed around her son's neck. Reese was then given a six-gun salute.

"He would have loved it," his widow later said.

"He was a common guy and a humble guy," explained old family friend Bob Shaw. "And it's the way a soldier would want to be buried."

In all his years in the Civil War group, Reese chose never to rise to officer's rank. He wanted to be a common soldier until the end.

At the end of June, Cunanan's mother MaryAnn returned quietly to National City, California, a working-class suburb of San Diego.

She knew all about her son's alleged crimes from visiting FBI investigators, who'd already been to see her in Illinois, and she feared he might one day come home.

MaryAnn was given an armed guard after her son committed his third murder. She told investigators that while she still loved her son dearly, she worried he might have a grudge against her.

She recalled to detectives how Cunanan had hit her on a number of occasions when he suffered huge mood swings that she thought had been brought on by his stressful lifestyle and drug abuse. She said that her son earned his living by working as a male prostitute. Investigators noted that she said it very coldly.

But despite all this, MaryAnn still had photos of Andrew displayed prominently in the sitting room of her small apartment.

Her life was full of contradictions.

Thirteen

KING OF THE CATWALK

On the surface, fashion designer Gianni Versace's life-style appeared to consist of glamorous models, immense wealth, private jets, and never-ending praise.

That world may well have also included alleged links with the Mafia, granite-faced bodyguards in reflective shades, vain young men in tight black leather jeans, even upmarket drug dealers and their overdressed women, but that all just came with the job.

For that questionable lifestyle was not the complete picture by any means. Gianni Versace was also a sensitive character, who was passionately interested in art, archaeology, and music.

He was touchingly flattered to be asked to design costumes for some of the world's most famous opera houses. He considered those projects as the light of his life.

For Versace would always remain the ambitious boy from Southern Italy's impoverished, Mafia-dominated Reggio di Calabria, brought up in a hardworking devoutly Roman Catholic family, suffocated by the love of an overly doting mother.

Versace's father, who made a living selling bottles of the methane gas many southerners used for cooking, was an authoritarian and distant figure. The two never got on, leaving the way for his far warmer and influential mother.

Certain aspects of this sound very similar to the upbringing of one Andrew Cunanan.

Versace's homosexuality set him apart in southern Italy. But his talent and drive took him north to fame, riches, and their often inevitable corruptions.

The story Versace told most often about his childhood was how his mother would take him to Communion past a Mob-run brothel in the little Italian town where he grew up. The girls would be hanging out of the windows or sitting on the steps. Versace's mother would order her son to close his eyes. He pretended to do so. But, of course, he peeked.

This, he later announced, was how his concept of female beauty was conceived. It was upfront, forbidden, and very flashy.

Those who knew Versace say that he was very shy at first but as he got used to people, he let his natural warmth show, never taking offense when criticized for designing clothes that were often accused of being vulgar and demeaning to women.

Single-handedly, Versace shifted fashion along a different path as his label gained strength in the 1980s. It was a path that many feminists believed set women back many years by depicting them as sexual toys.

By offering women's sexuality on such a sartorial plate, said the critics, his clothes implied that sexual availability was the most important thing any woman had to bargain with. It was, said the feminists, a fashion that completely portrayed a contempt for women. This was completely at odds with what Versace actually claimed. He had always insisted he loved women.

Commercially, high-class hooker style was the best thing that could have happened to Gianni Versace. Before that dramatic switch, he had been just another successful Italian designer among many, at best a crown prince to Giorgio Armani's king of Milan.

Versace constantly thumbed his nose at those who said his fashion was the height of bad taste—as many did when he showed his sadomasochistic collection at one big fashion show. He had been there before. His linebacker-shouldered, studded leathers and florid prints enthralled as many as it appalled.

And by the mid-1990s, the Versace label was dominating the world of fashion design. It had even become accessible to the man and woman in the street with $100 Versace jeans available.

Accessories, jeans, sportswear, childrenswear, homeware, and even beautifully glossy books all featured the famous Versace signature, a Medusa head.

In the history of fashion, Versace was not considered a great creator; he broke no molds. On the contrary, he forced women back into some old and dusty ones. But in their execution, his clothes were stunningly beautiful, their impact undeniable.

Versace's photograph, in the company of pop stars and beautiful actresses, graced the covers of magazines and newspapers virtually every week of the year. The quasi-cinematic myth had become a reality.

Never was this more so than when Versace's business took off in the U.S. It was those classic hallmarks of his style—turning men into studs and women into hookers—that were so adored in America.

And that adoration in the U.S. led to Versace being considered a virtual emigrant in the eyes of his native Italians. But they were proud that he had made it in the biggest marketplace of all. By 1995, Versace had profits of $900 million a year.

Versace's clothes were the ones worn by Oscar nominees, supermodels, and divorced princesses. Those same celebrities flocked to his lavish parties, to be entertained at his palazzo in Milan, his villa on Lake Como, in Italy, or his sumptuous house in South Beach, Miami.

He made Trudi Styler's wedding dress for her marriage to Sting. He dressed Madonna, Tina Turner, Sly Stallone, Mike Tyson, Faye Dunaway, George Michael, Elton John, Prince and in a seesaw battle with his archrival Giorgio Armani, Eric Clapton.

Diana, Princess of Wales, became a convert to Versace when she attended a Pavarotti charity concert in Italy. One year, Versace even visited the princess's London home, Kensington Palace, to go through a selection of pieces from his spring/summer collection with her.

When rumors abounded that Versace had AIDS in 1995, the designer quickly dispelled the gossip by emerging from a cancer scare with his hair silvered, albeit diminished, and his creative powers intact. He had beaten a serious illness with typical determination.

After cancer was diagnosed, Versace even said: "There were a lot of tests and scans and treatments that were hard. But as I said, 'I'm very optimistic. I never fall down. I always fight.'"

Versace never appeared vulnerable to friends and relatives. He seemed protected, if only by the sense that modern fashion could not go on without him.

But another kind of protection, it was alleged, overshadowed the Versace business even when the label was launched back in the late 1970s. There seemed to be rather a lot of money being fed into it for such a modest-sized business. This gave rise to the inevitable whispers—always vigorously denied—about Mafia backing.

It was a rumor that would stay with the company for its entirety. The gossip was fuelled by Versace's habit of pushing journalists to accept overly generous gifts such as $1,500 leather jackets waiting in their hotel rooms when they arrived for a Versace fashion show or $750 handbags delivered to people's homes at Christmas.

On the party front, Versace was renowned for hosting the biggest and best in town. This would frequently consist of 500 people sitting down to a sumptuous six-course dinner in a palazzo decorated with $30,000 worth of flowers and every guest sent away with a pint-sized bottle of scent.

But the rumors about Versace's Mafia links persisted. When one of his biggest stores in the world was opened, one fashion expert dubbed it "the prettiest launderette in the world." This kind of sotto voce allusion to alleged Mob connections continued to dog Versace.

By the mid-nineties he was surrounded by bodyguards, and often travelled in Italy in a bulletproof car. Rarely, if ever, did he walk openly in the streets of Milan. Gianni Versace lived in fear of the Mafia.

He believed that he would eventually be kidnapped and killed by a ruthless and relatively new branch of the Mafia from his Calabrian homeland, the 'Ndragheta. Behind his back, they had been using his business to launder increasingly large amounts of money.

Versace confided in his secret fears to Frank Monte, a New York–based security consultant. He was drafted by Versace to try and solve the mystery of the Mob's possible involvement in his business.

"He wanted me to get the books and clean up the act," said Monte.

During one clandestine meeting with the designer on November 30, 1996, in Central Park, Versace talked to him about a "black hand" at work within his empire. He left the private investigator with no doubt that the Mob had made inroads into the Versace business, albeit without the cooperation of Versace himself.

Versace approached Monte in the first place because he

wanted a bodyguard while in New York because "he was scared there."

And at the root of his fears were the 'Ndragheta—the potent third force in the Italian criminal underworld after the Sicilian Cosa Nostra and the Neapolitan Camorra.

Monte later explained, "Versace wanted us to find out was happening."

Versace told Monte about a homosexual acquaintance called Guglielmo "Johnny" Gatto, who had kept handwritten ledgers of money that had been forced into the Versace system by the Mafia ever since the early days of the business.

That money was then "cleaned" so as to appear to be legitimate income. But it was repayable to the Mob, and therefore logged in special records kept by Gatto.

Versace believed that following a wrangle involving Gatto's personal affairs and gay lifestyle Gatto had felt betrayed and bitter and had stolen the ledgers. Now he was trying to blackmail Versace. He had already told the designer that unless he was paid a large sum he would take the papers to the Italian authorities.

"We are talking about millions and millions here," Versace told Monte.

"Is this millions of dollars or lire?"

Versace replied: "I'm talking about millions of dollars."

Shortly after that meeting, Gatto was run over and killed by a bus in Milan—at least that was the cause of death officially registered by the coroner.

Monte later revealed: "All our inquiries showed that he had been strangled before being run over by the bus."

The ledgers had disappeared without a trace after someone broke into Gatto's apartment and stole all the books.

Throughout Monte's inquiries on behalf of Versace, the fashion designer desperately tried to distance himself from the investigation.

Said Monte: "It's typical of these guys—when it gets hard, they don't want to know. They'll tell you all their problems and they want you to solve them, then wait for the bill. He didn't want to get involved."

But Monte never forgot the fear he could see in Versace's eyes during that last fateful meeting with the designer in Central Park on that wintry November day.

"Versace was very worried. He was scared about the threat of money-laundering and what that might bring with it. He was starting to understand that it wasn't just people having money to give for a bit of extra profit."

Monte even offered to design a special kit for Versace's briefcase with radio equipment so he could always be tracked in case someone did actually kidnap him. But the plan was never put into action.

However Versace's closest friends insisted that, at heart, Versace was family-oriented, easiest in the company of the families of his brother Santo and sister Donatella.

He liked to think of himself as an open, essentially simple man who had no secrets from anyone. He had become the first major designer to talk openly about his homosexuality.

Patriarchal, he may have been. Socially ambitious, he certainly was. Hungry for artistic recognition beyond the tawdry acclaim accorded a fashion designer—he was doubtless that too.

But Versace also had another, possibly fatal, side to his character.

He was drawn like a magnet to the society of weirdos, exhibitionists, and inverts who populated the area near his home in South Beach.

This was the world of leather, studs, big bikes, tattoos, and sadomasochistic paraphernalia of a deviant minority inhabiting a drug-fueled and violent side of society.

Versace's attraction to handsome young men may well have given his designs a raunchy, money-spinning edge. But it may also had led him down a one-way path to self-destruction.

WANTED BY THE FBI

Andrew Phillip Cunanan
Unlawful Flight to Avoid Prosecution - Murder

Race: White; Sex: Male; Height: 5'9" - 5'11"; Weight: 160-165 lbs.
Date of Birth: 8/31/69; Hair: Brown (short); Eyes: Brown; Wears glasses and/or contact lenses
CAUTION: CONSIDER ARMED AND DANGEROUS
Please contact the nearest FBI office if you have any information
on Andrew Phillip Cunanan.

The FBI distributed this flyer showing the many faces of Andrew Cunanan. *(AP/Wide World Photos)*

Top: Italian fashion designer Gianni Versace (right) and sister Donatella flank Elton John at the Council of Fashion Designers Award Gala at New York's Lincoln Centre. *(AP/Wide World Photos)*

Bottom: Gianni Versace gestures while being applauded by models including Naomi Campbell (left) in Paris at the end of his 1997 Spring-Summer haute-couture collections.

Top: Andrew Cunanan (left) in a 1987 high school yearbook photo from The Bishop's School in San Diego, California. The photo was for the school's 'Gentleman's club'.

Bottom: Andrew Cunanan at a high school dance in 1985.

(Jamie Lytle/SYGMA)

Another high school yearbook photo of Cunanan. The caption accompanying the photo in the yearbook reads 'most likely to be remembered'. *(AP/Wide World Photos)*

Top: Television crews set up outside Versace's mansion after the brutal shooting.*(AP/Wide World Photos)*

Bottom: The redpickup truck that Cunanan stole from his fourth victim, William Reese in southern New Jersey, is towed from a Miami Beach parking garage. *(AP/Wide World Photos)*

Above: Grief-stricken celebrities, including (left to right) Sting, his wife Trudy Styler, Princess Diana, and Elton John, gather together to mourn the passing of their friend Giannia Versace.

(AP/Wide World Photos)

Left: Flowers lie on the blood-stained steps of Gianni Versace's mansion in the Miami Beach Tuesday, July 15, 1997. Versace was gunned down on the steps walking home from the nearby New Café.

(AP/Wide World Photos)

Top: Andrew Cunanan's trail of terror came to an end in this Miami houseboat, where Cunanan was found dead.

(Jared Michaels/SIPA Press)

Bottom: Officials remove Cunanan's body from the Miami houseboat where the serial killer committed suicide with a single gunshot to the head.

(Savino/SIPA Press)

Fourteen

MEN ON A MISSION

On Saturday July 5, 1997, Gianni Versace hosted the launch of his autumn/winter collection in the basement of the Ritz Hotel, in Paris.

Here, twice a year, he closed down the health club and spread his catwalk over the subterranean swimming pool; members fumed and the fashion pack raved.

Untypically, this time, there were none of the supermodels who Versace himself had helped create; no Linda Evangelista, no Christy Turlington, no Kate Moss. Naomi Campbell, faithful to the end, was one of the stars and was selected by Versace himself to appear as the finale "bride" on the show.

But more important than any celebrity or supermodel was the presence in the front row of Versace's niece Allegra, nine, and nephew Daniel, six.

The boy was resplendent in a scaled-down Versace suit with his brogue-clad feet swinging a good six inches from the floor. They were the children of Versace's sister and muse, Donatella, and young heirs to the Versace empire.

Backstage after the show, Versace was, as ever, engulfed by a tidal wave of fashion kisses and congratulations. He kissed one fashion editor from a British newspaper and whispered in her ear: "I'm on another planet."

The words referred to his parade of futuristic chainmail that was part Crusader knight, part *Star Trek*.

Later that evening, Versace and Donatella hosted a party at the Ritz Club, attended by stars such as Demi Moore and Rupert Everett.

Within a few days they were on a private plane to Miami and his vast piazza on Ocean Drive, South Beach.

The mansion, Casa Casuarina, had originally been built in the twenties. It was a Shangri-La, nicknamed fashion's "Versailles," and converted at vast expense to meet the needs of Versace and his extended family.

This entourage included his close friend of twelve years, Antonio d'Amico, his older brother, Santo, the computer-brain who controlled the finances of the multimillion-dollar Versace empire, and Donatella with her children and American-born husband, Paul Beck, who between them master-minded the Versace advertising and promotional imagery.

Versace had first seen the Art Deco district of South Beach in the early 1980s when he designed outfits for Don Johnson in the *Miami Vice* TV series.

He later turned the only residential property on Ocean Drive into a memorial to Miami's elegance in the thirties. Employing an architect from Washington and designers from Italy, he bought and renovated the building in 1992. He spent $3.7 million alone razing a neighboring hotel to make way for the Italian garden and frescoed swimming pool.

Like everything Versace did, the house was built to be larger than life. "Come up with your wildest ideas and then go one further," he told the creative team behind the multimillion-dollar restoration of the mansion.

They obeyed, having become accustomed to the needs of a man who, in his Milan home, bathed in a Roman emperor's bath hewn from stone and slept in a fourteenth-century wooden bed draped with fur and surrounded by Old Masters depicting the martyrdom of Saint Sebastian.

The result was a mansion in South Beach that would have left Cecil B. DeMille open-mouthed. Gold and silver plates, towers of flowers, priceless furniture, pictures and sculpture. Versace lived like a prince in every sense of the word.

The house itself had been designed on the outside to look like Diego Columbus's sixteenth-century castle in Santo Domingo. Inside it was decorated à la Versace with leopard-skin ceilings, mosaics, and Picassos and Modiglianis.

Versace was entranced by the light, the colors, the life, and the perfectly sculptured bodies of the beach gods adorning the South Beach sidewalks.

"It was love at first sight," Versace told a local Miami TV show in the spring of 1997. "It's like the world should be today."

In its glorification of drug use and promiscuity, the area seemed an incredibly destructive throwback to the seventies when New York City plugged into an era of extreme permissiveness that drew gay men from around the world— Versace among them.

What seemed especially appealing about this demimonde was that other equally flamboyant fashion designers were leading from the front. Night after night in South Beach, a group of household fashion names could be seen hanging out with fellow bisexual or homosexual millionaires in a clique known as the Velvet Mafia.

Versace soon began to enjoy large quantities of cocaine and prowled the city's backroom bars where brutal, impersonal sex with total strangers was easily obtained.

The seventy-five-foot frontage of Versace's house looked onto Eleventh Street, a block from the popular Clevelander Bar, and its observatory tower faced the grassy park, palm trees, jogging path, and beach where Versace loved to walk.

For his fidelity to the Italian Gothic and Classical Renaissance, Versace even won a preservation award from the board of the Florida Trust. It was, he told friends, the only place where he could truly relax and feel safe.

Yet the house only had an iron gate to protect it from a

constant throng of bustling crowds on the sidewalk. Just that and a small paved courtyard separated his front door from the street.

Miami's other celebrity residents—Sylvester Stallone, Madonna, Cher, the Bee Gees, and Julio Iglesias—all lived far from prying eyes on heavily secured enclaves well off the main streets further up the coast.

Inevitably, Versace's house soon became one of the resort's main tourist attractions. Street traders even often sold T-shirts, sun hats, and fake Cuban cigars in front of the mansion.

It was renowned as the only celebrity house you could see inside when the front door opened.

Many could not understand why, with all his millions, Versace even lived on Ocean Drive with all the weirdos who walked up and down outside virtually day and night.

Some nights men with guns conducted drug deals just a few yards from the Versace house. The nearby gay bars were packed until three or four in the morning most nights.

Why didn't Versace buy a big place overlooking the water, away from the street?

By 1997, the beachfront area had become an oasis or fun and revelry—and widespread homosexuality—in a city where violence still stalked.

Versace loved to throw lavish parties at the Ocean Drive mansion. He told friends he felt uncomfortable hanging out at the nearby gay bars, some of which were only a few yards from his home.

But when his long-term live-in lover and personal trainer—Antonio d'Amico—was not in town he did make appearances at the seafront's gay bars and nightclubs.

At the Palace Grill, just next door to the Versace mansion, waiter Les Supernor, forty-two, often saw young guys with him. "They were always very good-looking. When he went to the beach or out to bars he would have guys with him. They looked like male models."

Versace would also pop into The Warsaw, a steaming nightclub also just a short distance from his mansion.

A Versace Room was even created at the club as a tribute to the designer. It featured hundreds of his photos on the walls.

Versace was renowned as a real party animal when he was in the mood.

He also liked to go out to the nearby Pizza in the Bang restaurant, where he'd often share a glass of wine with its owner Massimo Lucarini.

Lucarini even originally planned to buy the mansion to make a restaurant. Then Versace contacted him and begged him to drop his plans. "I thought it was better for Miami to have Versace than another restaurant, so I said 'yes,' " Lucarini later recalled.

At 4:40 P.M. on July 7, 1997, Andrew Cunanan, who had already been on the FBI's Ten Most Wanted List for more than a month, sold one of Lee Miglin's gold coins at a Miami Beach pawn shop called Cash on the Beach.

To complete the transaction, which was conducted through two inches of bulletproof Plexiglas, he showed store manager Vivian Oliva identification, including his U.S. passport, and, on a required form, wrote his real name and current address—the Normandy Plaza hotel, which was just a block from the pawn shop. He also provided a print of his right thumb.

But when Oliva offered him $190 for the coin, Cunanan demanded, "Why are you giving me so little? It cost me so much."

The offer was upped by $10 and Cunanan appeared to go away a reasonably happy man.

The next day, July 8, Oliva followed procedure and mailed

a copy of the receipt to the Miami Beach Police Department. In order to help catch criminals, Florida law required pawn shop brokers to forward information about their transactions to their local police department within twenty-four hours.

The receipt arrived at the Miami Beach Police Department on either July 9 or 10, almost two months after Cunanan had killed his last known victim.

But because that particular department did not have an automated procedure to handle such paperwork, it sat in a pile on a clerk's desk for more than a week.

A couple of days later in Miami Beach, on the main Collins Avenue thoroughfare linking the city with Fort Lauderdale, Cunanan was spotted by tennis pro David Todini.

The cross-country spree killer was wandering along the sidewalk near the racket club where Todini worked.

He recognized Cunanan from his appearance on *America's Most Wanted* TV show and called the police, but by the time they arrived the man had gone.

Andrew Cunanan seemed to have a lot of good luck besides a murderous determination to survive.

Gianni Versace had already decided he would spend much more time at his Miami Beach house. The previous summer, as he recovered from surgery to remove a small tumor behind an ear, he confided as much to a former business partner, Roberto Devorik, as they watched a performance by Luciano Pavarotti together.

"I need to cut my pace," Versace told his old friend. "Now I had my tumor removed, I realize I have to start enjoying my houses instead of just seeing them in magazines. I have to quiet down my life and I have to enjoy more my privacy."

It was with that pledge in mind that Gianni Versace and

his entourage arrived in Miami on Saturday July 12, 1997.

Exhausted from that blur of European fashion shows, Versace intended to laze about his villa, watching videos and reading.

Fifteen

BEWITCHED

On the evening of Monday July 14, 1997, Andrew Cunanan spent forty-five minutes with a travel agent next to the Normandy Plaza Hotel. He pored over travel maps and seemed, according to the staff, very distracted.

Cunanan was anxiously trying to decide his next move.

He then went on to eat and wandered the South Beach area thinking about what he was going to do.

Lastly, he checked on Bill Reese's red Chevy pickup. Its windshield was covered in parking tickets, but there was no sign of anyone watching it. Cunanan surmised that the vehicle had not been tracked down by authorities.

Cunanan got back to his hotel room about 8:30 that evening. He had been staying alone in the hotel for the best part of two months. It was a sparse place to call a temporary home but it served a purpose. The hotel staff had left him in peace, but he was worried about how he was going to find the money to pay for his room.

Even though it was night, Miami heat combined with the never ending fender-to-fender traffic had left the smell of smog drifting through the room.

Cunanan had carefully avoided any conversation with his neighbors on the third floor of the Normandy Plaza. The nearest other hotel rooms had changed hands at least a dozen times and he knew they'd not taken much notice of him.

Cunanan flicked on the lights in his room and looked around to check that no one had been in. His few clothes lay thrown across the bed and the floor where he had left them earlier that evening.

Satisfied that he was alone in the room, Cunanan went to the bathroom, took a long shower and washed his hair. He then laid out the clothes he wanted to wear for his prowl around the Ocean Drive gay bars and clubs that evening.

Then he carefully shaved the sides of his head to give himself a modest Mohawk-style haircut. It was an essential step if he were to continue evading the authorities.

The hotel hair drier had a plastic cap and hose. He put on the cap and, while he dried, he thumbed through the latest copy of *Vogue* magazine he'd picked up at the News Cafe earlier that day.

The leather and sadomasochistic nature of some high fashion intrigued him. The line between sadistic pornography and everyday trendsetting seemed to be getting thinner and thinner.

As he read he felt a twinge of excitement. He swivelled the reading lamp to be able to read more clearly. Outside the sound of the traffic began to fade, but every now and again he heard someone laughing from the sidewalk.

Cunanan then took out the .40 caliber handgun and began the laborious routine of cleaning it. He got cotton swabs out and carefully brushed every crevice in the weapon.

Six Golden Sabre bullets lay on the table in front of him.

Finally, he stood up and walked to the door to make sure it was locked. Then he loaded the gun carefully and deliberately, safe in the knowledge that no one could walk in on this very intimate scene.

Cunanan then put the gun down on the bedside table and walked to the window of the room where he looked down at the people on the sidewalk below and across the road to the beach. Cunanan carefully closed the tatty drapes over the windows to ensure that there wasn't even a sliver of light coming through them.

He turned out the lights and lay back on the bed and thought about his next move. Overhead a rusty fan spun gently around, providing a slight breeze.

When Cunanan closed his eyes he perhaps thought of his childhood, his father's discipline, the religious fanaticism of his mother. This then merged into the sadomasochistic scenes of torture and degradation in San Francisco.

Then his mind wandered to the deaths of Jeff Trail and David Madson. He pictured them alive. That satisfied his blood lust. He felt he'd done a service for them.

Sometime in the future he would be hailed as a savior, not a killer.

His eyes closed as he drifted into a semiconscious sleep, still aware of the noises outside but his mind escaping into a kaleidoscope of imagery.

The handcuffs, the other instruments of torture. The looks on those men's faces as they beat him. The brief encounters in alleys, restrooms, even in the corner of a dimly lit club.

Then one image suddenly became steadier and stronger. It was him. Gianni Versace. They were being introduced at the opera. He held onto his hand as they spoke a few words in Italian.

Cunanan awoke with a start.

He sat up and decided the time had come to put the final touches to his plan.

The heavy drum and bass beat in The Twist nightclub had just reached its peak when the DJ looked over in Andrew Cunanan's direction. There was a flicker of recognition on his face. Cunanan couldn't tell if he knew him or whether it was just part of the rules of the game for picking a casual friend in one of the South Beach's best known gay clubs.

In fact Cunanan's appearance in the club on three nights over the previous week had drawn the attention of many. As the manager would later comment: "He had these amazing Bette Davis eyebrows that made him kinda memorable."

Andrew Cunanan had no idea that there was a video camera high in the corner of the ceiling of the main dance floor area of The Twist recording his presence on the premises.

Club regulars soon noticed the good-looking man in his mid-twenties who seemed to be alone.

"He wasn't giving off any vibes. Seemed to have a lot on his mind besides finding a new partner," one regular later recalled.

Cunanan was on a manhunt. He wanted to find Gianni Versace and meet him face-to-face. Stark though the contrast was between their lives, the lust they shared for the high life had convinced Cunanan that he had a special bond with the world-famous designer.

Cunanan looked very different from those photos on the FBI most wanted posters. His hair was now shaved up at the sides and he had acquired a tan from spending a few hours each day at the beach. He was trimmer than when he first arrived in Miami. He was ready.

He remained convinced the so-called king of fashion Gianni Versace would remember following their meetings in 1990 in San Francisco.

Cunanan had already established that Versace was a regular at The Twist and he was quite prepared to sit it out. He knew that the fashion designer had been in town since the weekend because he'd seen him go into his house from his vantage point on the beach.

Cunanan had actually spent the two previous nights at all the hangouts where he thought Versace might appear but to no avail.

He was going to give it one more night and then attempt to contact Versace some other way if he failed.

The Twist was a popular hang-out for fifty-year-old Versace. Whenever he was in the club, the DJ would usually make an announcement and the crowd would crane for a glimpse of the great man as, flanked by an entourage of tall blond, flawlessly beautiful men, he would slowly make his entrance, his eyes flicking from side to side with the hauteur of a Renaissance prince.

Cunanan knew from the fashion magazines he read so avidly that Versace was a fun merchant. Who else would equip his house with an outsize bed and a shower with room for eight people? From his observatory he could gaze across the Twelfth Street nude beach where youths dressed only in swimming briefs played volleyball or lazed suggestively in the pink sand.

Cunanan knew all about this side of South Beach life as he had spent a few nights over the previous two months attending dance-until-after-dawn beach parties where a big attraction was men in sequined and feathered drag. Some of the partygoers told Cunanan how Versace always showed up at these functions if he was in town and how he loved playing with the boys.

Over those two months Cunanan had become more and more convinced that Versace would help him in his time of need. After all, they had connected so well all those years previously.

One modeling agent told Cunanan in The Twist that night how Versace—who in every club would always be on the edge of the dance floor staring at the object of his desire and mouthing ''I'm Versace''—was reckless and relentless in his promiscuity.

It was easy for Cunanan to stake out Versace until he made an appearance. In fact, he probably would have got to him much earlier if he hadn't been at those fashion shows in Europe.

Versace didn't show that evening in The Twist and Andrew Cunanan finally moved onto another club called Liquid.

Dressed in clean white T-shirt and black jeans, Cunanan approached a pair of the club's performing drag queens and tried to strike up a conversation. Most patrons ignored the drag queens or teased them. But Cunanan earnestly told them that he was a political science major new in town.

But once again there was no sign of Versace.

Cunanan's final port of call that evening and early morning was the KGB Club, which he entered on Collins Avenue through a red velvet curtain drawn across the front door.

Once inside, at a cost of $10, there was a blast of sound, heat and sweat; dancers jerked robotlike to the jungle music. It was so dark inside that, at the back, a man was standing with a flashlight pointing to the relevant door of the restrooms.

Some time after entering the club, Cunanan was directed to the men's room, and as he entered a figure emerged dressed as an eighteenth-century boudoir courtesan. He was wearing a blond powdered wig, heavy makeup and a long, sky-blue dress.

Robert was one of the club's most regular customers and Cunanan asked him if Versace was in the KGB that evening.

"I'm a friend of Versace," Cunanan anxiously told Robert.

"Yeah, sure," replied Robert, who didn't believe him because he'd only ever seen Versace in the company of tall blond boys.

Sixteen

COUNTDOWN

T he start of Tuesday July 15, 1997, had dawned like most
 on South Beach with blue skies, a light breeze and a
warm sun.

Walking to the News Cafe on Ocean Drive, was a regular
start-of-the-day routine for Gianni Versace, although on that
morning he seemed agitated and, unusually, he was alone.

Cafe hostess Stephanie Vanover, thirty, even noticed that
Versace approached the restaurant from the opposite, beach
side, of the street, which was unusual. She had actually seen
Versace walk right past the premises before crossing the
street and returning "in a sort of loop."

Vanover later recalled: "It was almost as though he knew
someone was following him."

When Versace greeted Stephanie he was definitely less
relaxed than usual. At the counter of the restaurant's newstand, Versace spent $15.01 on five magazines: *Business
Week, Vogue, Entertainment Weekly, People* and *The New
Yorker*. He asked for *Time* magazine as well, but the store
did not have it in stock.

Just then he noticed News Cafe manager Tony Puche
nearby.

"Good morning, it is a beautiful day," the fashion designer told Puche.

Then Versace departed, strolling past a group of tourists staking out places on the beach and beginning the four-block walk to his home at 1116 Ocean Drive.

Even though the temperature was heading for the high eighties, Versace walked off much faster than usual past the pastel colored Art Deco hotels that lined the street.

As he dodged rollerbladers, Versace glanced up at the glass-fronted South Beach gym above the popular Clevelander Bar where sweating, muscular men were going through their daily exercises.

Farther along the street Versace passed the product of such gyms, young men with rippling muscles, wearing only shorts, who used the ten-block Ocean Drive boulevard as a fashion ramp to show off their biceps.

Shortly before nine A.M., Versace pulled out his keys to unlock the black wrought-iron gates to his palatial, multimillion-dollar home.

Just then a man in his mid-twenties suddenly approached. It was Andrew Cunanan. He was dressed in gray muscle T-shirt, black shorts, black baseball cap, and tennis shoes. There was an exchange of words. Witnesses later claimed that both men were cursing at each other in Italian.

Cunanan took the .40 caliber out from his backpack and shot Gianni Versace in the head. The designer fell as the first bullet hit him. Then Cunanan coolly and calmly bent down to put a second bullet into his skull.

"I heard pow, pow, and I ducked on the ground," local restaurant dishwasher Romeo Jacques, nineteen, later recalled.

Versace's sunglasses, sandals, wallet, newspapers, and magazines fell by the side of his body. They were stained in his blood.

Cunanan then pocketed his gun and walked toward a crowd of nearby shoppers, leaving his victim dying on the coral-pink stone steps to the mansion.

At that moment Antonio d'Amico, Versace's longtime companion ran from the house and chased Cunanan down an alley. When Cunanan turned and pointed his gun in d'Amico's direction, he ducked and turned around to run back toward his dying lover. He found the designer lying on the steps, his face up, blood pouring everywhere. Versace shook a little. Then he was still.

Unknown to Cunanan his dash down a back alley behind the $200-a-night Tides Hotel was recorded by a security video camera.

Once Cunanan was sure that no-one was on his tail he went into the parking lot where he'd left Bill Reese's pickup truck, put on a new set of clothes, left the shorts and T-shirt he had been wearing in a pile and walked away. He'd decided to abandon the truck and flee on foot after seeing police officers investigating a car accident near the parking lot.

In his pocket were the four remaining Golden Sabre .40 caliber bullets.

Within an hour of the shooting, police received reports that four cars had been stolen from the area.

Eddie Bianchi was at a nearby rollerblade store when he heard the two shots. Bianchi rushed out of the store and saw Gianni Versace lying on the steps of his nearby house. He was face-up and shaking. There was a man walking in and out of the house in a daze. There was also a woman screaming, "I saw him! I saw him!"

Bianchi later recalled, "We heard two shots. I saw people running. Gianni was on the stairs. He was shot twice in the head. We were trying to help him but realized it was too late. He was lying there and he was so badly shot you could see his open head. It was really awful."

Barry Elkins, who lived nearby, said: "I heard two pops—bang, bang. Then he fell to the ground and the gunman ran off."

Police and paramedics arrived at the scene within three minutes. They bravely went through the motions to try and revive Versace as the ambulance rushed to Miami's Jackson Memorial Hospital.

The two shots at close range had left Versace virtually unrecognizable and he actually died in the ambulance of heart failure. At the hospital's Ryder Trauma Center, doctors confirmed that Versace was dead from two shots in the back of the head.

The Dade County Medical Examiner was immediately ordered to carry out a speedy autopsy. Celebrity killings were a rarity even in gun-crazy Miami and this was a top priority.

Back at the scene of the murder, detectives quickly recovered two Golden Sabre .40 caliber cartridge cases from the steps.

Then one of the officers spotted a dead pigeon lying at the bottom of the steps, just a few feet from the body. Was it a symbol left by the killer or just a coincidence?

Among those magazines scattered on the steps to the mansion was *People*, which had just carried a profile of cross-country serial killer Andrew Cunanan.

Soon after the killing, hundreds of mourners gathered outside Versace's white-walled, red-roofed house. They lay bunches of flowers and tributes on the bloodied steps. Versace's sandals were still in the same position they had been after his body was removed. Later a county worker appeared at the scene and tried in vain to scrub the dried blood off the four front steps.

No one thought twice about the dark-haired young man who watched from behind the crowd as police investigators and forensic experts went in and out of the Versace mansion. It was just three hours after Versace was shot and Andrew Cunanan had returned to the scene of his crime to gloat.

Come and get me if you can.

At first, detectives believed that all the evidence pointed to the death of Versace as some kind of Mob-inspired hit or a former lover taking cold-blooded revenge.

His alleged connections were an open secret after all.

From behind yellow police cordon tape, reporters gathered for a press conference on the South Beach sidewalk.

Miami police chief Richard Barreto announced to reporters: "He was shot twice in the back of the head. I believe that he was targeted. This man was lying in wait for him. It was an execution-style murder."

Police remained completely puzzled by the dead pigeon found close to Versace's body.

A spokesman said: "We do not know if the bird was a coincidence or some kind of symbol."

Rumors of a Mafia-commissioned hit on Versace were soon gaining momentum.

Within minutes of Versace's death, Jonny Williams, editor of *He-Lines* fashion magazine and a close friend of Versace's was telling reporters: "There are a lot of people who could have killed him. He was probably one of the most powerful people in fashion, and certain people don't like anyone being that powerful. There are rumors about who really owned the company. We called him the godfather of fashion for an article. Someone I met in Italy two weeks ago laughed at the headline and said 'perfect.' My immediate reaction when I heard about his death was that it was something to do with the Mafia. I've heard rumors that go back thirteen years."

But Miami police were soon considering other motives behind the killing. One source told journalists, "Mr. Versace was openly homosexual and could often be seen on the beach being oiled down by young men.

"We will naturally be questioning members of the gay community."

*   *   *

The contents of a garbage bag dropped while the killer was running south on Miami Springs Avenue yielded the baseball cap, socks, and jeans he was wearing when he killed Versace. Police didn't immediately realize it, but these items were actually Andrew Cunanan's calling cards, tokens of a boundless arrogance.

Witnesses quickly came forward to say that they'd seen a man fitting the description of the killer running into a parking lot three blocks from Versace's house just a few minutes after the killing.

Shortly after this, on level 3B of that parking lot a red pickup was discovered, its windshield almost entirely covered with parking tickets. Police quickly established it had been stolen by a suspected serial killer called Andrew Cunanan from his fourth victim, cemetery caretaker Bill Reese.

Yet another passport and a Bank of America check bearing Cunanan's name were found in the pickup, repeating a pattern of clues to his identity left at the scene of all his earlier murders. They also found eyeglasses, a jacket, and an expensive wallet, all belonging to victim number three Lee Miglin. Investigators hoped the vehicle would also contain Cunanan's fingerprints.

Investigators discovered from the mass of parking tickets that the vehicle had been in the lot since June 6. Why wasn't it reported to authorities earlier?

On closer examination of the newspaper clippings of the case found in the truck, detectives stumbled upon a chilling handwritten list of celebrities' names. At the top of that list were Madonna and singer Julio Iglesias. Both had huge mansions just a short distance from Versace's beachfront home. They were immediately informed by investigators to take special security precautions within hours of the killing of Versace.

The hit list also included oil heir Gordon Getty, San Francisco socialite Harry de Widt, and a number of wealthy doctors and lawyers in the Miami area.

Cunanan even referred in his list to the "bad attitude" of celebrities for his own failure to break into movies as an actor.

Police also found Cunanan had written his name in his own blood inside the truck.

Come and get me if you can . . .

Seventeen

AMERICA'S MOST WANTED

Within hours of the Versace shooting, police had pieced together enough evidence to announce that Andrew Cunanan was their number-one suspect.

Miami police chief Richard Barreto told a mass of reporters: "Cunanan has to be considered extremely dangerous and armed at this time. He is known to have an affluent clientele. He is well-dressed and articulate."

Barreto also revealed that the FBI had immediately been called into the investigation.

"This is because of the striking similarities between the Versace case and other murders across the country where Cunanan is the chief suspect," one bureau source told numerous reporters shortly after the Versace killing. "He fits the profile to a tee. He is a one-man killing machine. We have known for some time that Cunanan has been killing at random."

FBI chief Paul Philip was even more blunt about Cunanan when he made a chilling announcement to the public.

"Nobody's safe. We've been looking for this man since April. Please help us put him in jail."

But with no previous convictions and no distinguishing scars or marks, the FBI knew full well that Andrew Cunanan could still prove incredibly elusive.

To add to their frustration, the FBI conceded that there had been hundreds of sightings of Cunanan all over the country since his previous murder of Bill Reese in Pennsville, New Jersey.

However the majority of those sightings had been in Florida where the bureau had distributed 2,000 posters over the previous two weeks.

Now Gianni Versace's murder had given the case a much larger profile and the FBI immediately set up a telephone line for anyone with information about Cunanan or Versace's killing.

As news of Versace's killing spread across the globe, the fashion designer's famous friends began an immense outpouring of grief.

Diana, Princess of Wales, said, "I am devastated by the loss of a great and talented man."

Star client and friend Elton John said, "I am devastated to have lost one of my closest friends, who I loved so much. We were so close that it is like a large part of my life has died with him."

Elton John's companion, David Furnish, said that Versace continually sent faxes to his friends "letting you know he was looking and listening" even flying to New York just to attend a premiere of Furnish's TV documentary on Elton John called "Tantrum and Tiaras."

"If I had to sum Gianni up in one word, it's passion," said Furnish. "I never met someone with such a passion for life, and beauty, and living. He enjoyed life, devoured it, and gave it all back to the world. He is someone who was doing what he was born to do and he got so much pleasure from it."

Grief-stricken supermodel Naomi Campbell echoed the emotion of millions when she paid tribute to Versace. With tears pouring down her cheeks, she said: "I feel pain and anger for what has happened. It's a crime and a disgrace and it should never have happened. I feel pain for Gianni's whole family. Now no one's ever going to see him again. It's not fair."

Versace's brother Santo said: "He was a good man. And he was killed by a madman."

Even Versace's rivals were gracious in their tributes.

Calvin Klein said: "Gianni created a style which will survive his death."

Karl Lagerfeld said Versace "helped create Italian fashion."

Alex Penelas, mayor of Metro Dade County, which covers the greater Miami area, said: "Versace embodied the energy and vibrance of South Beach. To a large extent, it was Versace's presence that brought this community fame and fortune. For all that we can be eternally grateful."

Meanwhile, the impromptu shrine outside Versace's mansion continued to grow. Flowers and candles marked the spot where he'd been shot.

And at the heart of Milan's bustling fashion world—where the designer king first made his mark in the 70s—the windows of one shop were stripped of their usual finery within hours of the news of Versace's death.

Instead, a simple, black-edged card read "Closed for mourning."

At first, Versace's distraught sister Donatella, forty, refused to believe that her famous brother was dead—until she viewed his body at a Miami mortuary.

Donatella was flown by private jet from Italy immediately after being told of Versace's death.

A friend who was present with her as she was shown Versace's bullet-ridden face said she could barely stand.

"She couldn't grasp the horrific truth until she saw him for herself. It wasn't a pretty sight," explained the friend.

After leaving the morgue, she headed for her brother's vast mansion where the family had bravely decided to stay the night as a tribute to the slain designer.

Meanwhile news of Versace's death continued to stun the world.

The usually conservative *New York Times* gave the story heavy prominence on its front page.

VERSACE, FASHION INNOVATOR, SLAIN IN MIAMI BEACH

The paper reported:

> *MIAMI BEACH, July 15—Gianni Versace, the fashion designer who rejuvenated the industry by tapping into the energy of popular culture, was gunned down and killed this morning as he opened the gate of his palatial South Beach home here. The police said the killing was the work of a man wanted for murders in three states.*

Britain's news-hungry tabloid daily newspapers blasted the story across all their front pages with vast banner headlines like GAY ASSASSIN SHOT VERSACE and VERSACE-EXECUTED BY GAY SLAYER.

The Daily Mail, in London referred to a "sensational twist as FBI name serial killer as sole suspect."

The paper went on to report:

> *A gay serial killer was named early today as the suspected murderer of designer Gianni Versace.*
>
> *Andrew Cunanan, 27, is believed to have already killed at least four men and is on the FBI's most wanted list . . .*

The day after Versace's killing, yacht owner Guillermo Volpe found cushions moved and two newspapers, including the Italian *Corriere della Sera* headlining the Versace murder, on the deck of his vessel docked in Indian Creek, Miami Beach. It was just forty blocks from the scene of Gianni Versace killing.

It looked to Volpe like clear evidence that someone had been sleeping on the deck the previous evening.

Normally Volpe would have taken little notice but what with the alert over Versace killer Andrew Cunanan he thought he'd better call the police.

They fingerprinted the boat and departed and he heard nothing more about it.

Also on the day after Versace's killing, Cash on the Beach pawn shop manager Vivian Oliva called police after hearing Cunanan's name and seeing his photograph on the news. The name sounded vaguely familiar, she later told an officer. She then checked her records and put two and two together.

Detectives arrived at the pawn shop just a block from the Normandy Plaza Hotel in double quick time and took the thumbprint and the receipt left by Cunanan.

The gold coin that had been pawned at the shop belonged to Cunanan's third victim Lee Miglin.

Oliva wondered why the police had not responded to the receipt signed by Cunanan that she had sent—as the law required—to Miami Beach police the previous Thursday.

If they had reacted to it, then Cunanan would have been apprehended and Gianni Versace would not have been killed.

Dozens of officers then raided the Normandy Plaza Hotel, as it had been named on the pawn shop receipt as Cunanan's place of residence. But within half an hour of searching a number of rooms they concluded that Cunanan had lied about where he was staying. They insisted to reporters there had been no evidence that he'd even spent a night in the hotel.

The FBI's new wanted poster for Andrew Cunanan perfectly illustrated the problems facing investigators in their hunt for the serial killer.

From the photos featured it was clear he was a chameleon, changing faces and personas as often as most people change clothes.

The photographs said it all.

At times, he appeared a fresh-faced preppy, wearing horn-rimmed glasses and chinos.

At others, a military man, stern-faced with hair closely cropped.

Then, a darkly handsome model, striking a sexy, dramatic pose.

Cunanan had avoided the dragnet for so long because he had the ability to melt into the background.

Just forty-eight hours after Versace's murder, Andrew Cunanan proved he had not vanished into thin air—by telephoning a friend in San Diego.

"I need a passport. You know anyone who might have one I could use?" Cunanan talked as if it was a perfectly normal request.

He also made it clear that he was intending to travel abroad.

Cunanan then asked his friend about a number of mutual acquaintances on the East Coast. He never once mentioned the shooting of Versace and ended the call when it became clear that his friend could not help him.

In the Philippine town of Plaridel, where Cunanan's father Modesto lived, he was questioned by local police, who wanted to know if his son had tried to contact him lately.

Modesto insisted his son was not the killer of Gianni Versace or any of his other alleged victims.

"My son is not like that," Modesto told the police. "He had a Catholic upbringing. He was an altar boy."

But there were hints of the family's rough streak. Modesto's neighbors said that the older Cunanan had recently burned the clothes of his live-in girlfriend after a fight.

Modesto now lived in a rented room in a working-class neighborhood but he insisted: "How could my son associate with the highest-class of society? Andrew is only a middle-class person."

Just then Filipino police officer, Inspector Celidonio Morales, asked Modesto Cunanan: "Some people say you have a sugar plantation?"

"If I say I have a sugar plantation in Alaska, you can accept it?"

Later, in another interview, Modesto Cunanan admitted he'd hit his son when he was young but insisted: "It was nothing special. I am a services guy. I respect discipline and I expected my kids to abide by my code of discipline as well."

In America, it was gradually dawning on citizens that five men had been murdered by one man apparently hell-bent on destroying as many lives as he could.

The Washington Post seemed to sum up the feeling of the nation in an article headlined LIFE STORIES:

Five Men Were Murdered. But That Was Only the Ending.

An architect and a gas company manager in Minneapolis. A millionaire in Chicago. A cemetery groundskeeper in New Jersey. A fabulously successful fashion designer in Miami.

Five men are dead, and investigators are seeking the fugitive Andrew Cunanan in the slayings. One reportedly was his former lover and one was a friend, the others either acquaintances or strangers.

A serial killer, it appears, has been wandering the

country. People are grasping at theories, trying to explain away the seeming randomness of the violence. Surely there was a way to make sense of all this—and, in doing so, keep it at a distance.

But whatever connections the police may eventually uncover ultimately do not matter. The meaning of lives is not in their end, even when that end is a major media event. People should not be reduced to a step in a trail of murder, a clue in the story of a manhunt.

The article then outlined the tragic deaths of the other four victims just to remind the world that Cunanan was responsible for more than just the slaying of a legendary fashion world figure.

South Beach rollerblade store owner Eddie Bianchi summed up the local reaction to Versace's killing when he said just hours after the murder: "All this is awful. I was proud to show people the house of Gianni Versace, the beautiful house he had rebuilt. Now you feel embarrassed. It's the crime house."

In New Jersey, Dee Blake couldn't believe the gall of Andrew Cunanan.

She was watching TV news coverage of the murder of Gianni Versace when she saw the red 1995 Ford pickup truck that belonged to her former employee, Bill Reese, being towed away by the police.

"I'm absolutely amazed that he would be riding that truck," said Dee Blake. "Obviously, he's somebody who is cold, calculating, who has no regard for human life. It's frightening."

Eighteen

FEAR ON THE STREETS

Not far from the parking lot where Andrew Cunanan abandoned Bill Reese's red pickup on South Beach, Interstate 95 begins its route north back up the Florida coastline.

Banded by blaring signs, fast-food outlets, and automotive services, four lanes carry traffic up along the turnpike toward coastal resorts such as Hollywood, Fort Lauderdale, and beyond.

On the evening of July 15—the day after Gianni Versace was gunned down in cold blood—Andrew Cunanan was seen drinking at the Choices Steakhouse, in the city of Boca Raton, forty-five miles north of Miami.

News of the Versace killing was still being reported around the clock on TV, but Choices didn't have a set on the premises. That might explain why Cunanan chose it as a safe spot to refresh himself before heading further north.

FBI agents raided the restaurant after a tip-off later that evening, but Cunanan had long since gone and, frustratingly, no one had seen if he was driving a car. He just seemed to disappear into thin air.

Meanwhile Miami investigators were becoming increasingly convinced that Versace had recognized his killer.

This chance moment probably meant the designer signed his own death warrant because Cunanan knew he had to be killed in order to protect his liberty.

For that reason they were very anxious to gain full access to the Versace mansion on Ocean Drive.

Versace's family were not being particularly helpful as they refused to allow the police to search the house until two and a half days after the murder. Later, it was claimed this was due to a misunderstanding between federal authorities and the family's lawyer, but it certainly did not help speed up the police investigation.

As more than four hundred police and FBI agents followed up every reported sighting of Cunanan, much of the search was concentrating on tourist and homosexual haunts in Miami Beach and all over South Florida.

Police began distributing tens of thousands of leaflets featuring six photographs of the suspect in different disguises. These pictures had originally been given to the police following the murder of victim number two David Madson. But it was only now that the FBI felt the case warranted carrying all the photos on one poster.

Investigators also put out an APB to every police force in the country to try and trace any cars stolen over the previous few days in case Cunanan might be the culprit. They remained convinced that Cunanan may have been involved in one of those four car thefts in Miami Beach shortly after the Versace killing.

Miami's airports and docks police were also on constant alert.

A spokesman for the Florida Department of Law Enforcement said that the pursuit had yielded dozens of leads but they omitted to mention that none had led them to Andrew Cunanan, now the most wanted serial killer in U.S. history.

Miami district FBI chief Paul Philip even modified his initial chilling alert announcement on Cunanan. Twelve hours after his first warning he said: "We must catch this guy. Cunanan is armed and not just a threat to the gay community."

Miami detectives spent hours on the day after Versace's death studying videotape from security cameras at the News Cafe and other stores on Ocean Drive.

One cafe customer came forward and said he thought he'd seen Cunanan on the premises minutes before Versace was shot. But the videotapes showed no evidence of this.

Police and FBI officers continued working around the clock, chasing down sightings of serial killer Cunanan. But he was still proving incredibly elusive.

Metro Dade police reported they had more than 600 tipster calls as the reward for Cunanan's capture reached $65,000.

Unconfirmed sightings put Cunanan strolling in Key West, drinking beer in Florida City, at a Fort Lauderdale Dunkin Donuts, and enjoying the ponies at Hialeah racetrack—all at the same time. Other sightings were reported from New York, South Carolina, Arkansas, and Minnesota.

Some of Versace's associates in South Beach started talking about how the designer often went prowling for boys when the urge took his fancy. They claimed that the designer was frequently seen in the company of young men—but they were usually blond.

Lazaro Zubiadul, who described himself as "the queen of Miami Beach" said: "Versace liked blond guys, beautiful guys, fashion guys."

From the photographs of Cunanan, he said, it was difficult to believe he knew the dark-haired man. "Not his type. Not at all."

Most police and FBI officials remained convinced that Cunanan was still holed up in South Florida.

At The Twist nightclub that Cunanan had visited at least three times before Versace's murder, staff handed over security video camera footage in the hope it might show the wanted killer.

Inside the club, Miami police questioned patrons for further evidence that could help them find Cunanan. Regulars, none of whom earlier had recognized their close brush with death, racked their brains for a single memory of the suspected serial killer.

"It's just so scary to think he was in here and we didn't realize," explained one patron, Jimmy Valdez.

Across America, so-called serial killer experts were airing their views on Cunanan and predicting his next move.

"This guy is very dangerous, but he is nowhere near panicking," said William Tafoya, a former FBI officer. "Cunanan walked away from the last murder, apparently feeling as though he had nothing to worry about. Just think of it: law enforcement officials up and down the coast are redfaced. He is getting a serious rush from all this attention. He's arrogant and manipulative. But more than anything, he's feeding his ego."

Miami police and FBI agents continued to press all Versace's family and friends about whether the Italian designer knew Cunanan before the killing.

Versace's longtime companion, Antonio d'Amico, told investigators there was no relationship between Versace and Cunanan.

But one FBI source said: "If they knew each other, he's not saying. We still believe there was a link between the two of them. We certainly have little else to go on at the moment."

One thing investigators had established was that the shots that killed three of Cunanan's victims—including Versace—all came from the same weapon, Jeff Trail's .40 caliber handgun.

* * *

Then on the afternoon of Wednesday, July 17, the hottest lead of all sent the FBI and police swarming all over a house near Miami International Airport.

Local police had earlier been alerted to the house when they responded to a burglar alarm. They found the front door unlocked and inside discovered the naked body of a Cuban exile, Dr. Silvio Alfonso who worked in a nearby health clinic. His trousers were around his ankles. He had been killed in the same way as Versace—execution-style with two bullets in his head. The room was caked in blood and ransacked.

The murder scene—a $200,000 single-story white-painted house with a swimming pool in the back yard—was less than ten miles from where Versace was gunned down.

And a man matching Cunanan's description was spotted fleeing the Miami Springs home of Alfonso; it looked liked the work of the most wanted man in America.

Police towed Alfonso's 1995 BMW to search it for evidence. Detectives were trying to learn from neighbors whether any other vehicle was parked in the driveway overnight.

Friends and colleagues of Alfonso said he arrived in Miami from Cuba around 1990, leaving behind a wife and two daughters. Neighbors said he had been renovating the house, expecting them to join him.

"He would send them money, clothes, whatever he could do to help them," said Reginald Bottari, a chiropractor for whom Alfonso worked after first arriving from Cuba.

Bottari described Alfonso as "a bright and gifted doctor."

Authorities said the suspect was white, five-foot-ten and in his twenties—the same general profile of Cunanan.

They suspected that Cunanan might have picked up his latest victim at a Miami gay bar and used his home as a hideout.

Police spokesman Patrick Brickman said: "Our men are

going to the scene because it's a homicide. They're going to look at anything that has any kind of similarity or any point of reference to the Versace investigation."

.The case set off a stampede of reporters from Versace's villa to the quiet tree-lined residential street of Alfonso's home near the airport.

A neighbor who heard the alarm told police she saw a man fitting Cunanan's description, dressed in a blue blazer and light-colored slacks, walking on the sidewalk away from the house.

On seeing the witness, the man dropped a black bag containing a pair of blue jeans. The victim's wallet was found a few blocks from the house.

Police also discovered Alfonso's beeper near the bag.

Cunanan was then also linked to another Miami Beach killing. Police were trying to determine whether he was responsible for the slaying of Casey Patrick Sigler.

Sigler, forty-one, was beaten to death inside his apartment at 1601 Lenox Avenue, South Beach, late on the evening of May 12 by a man matching Cunanan's description. There were also earlier reported sightings of Cunanan and Sigler at Flamingo Park, a well-known pickup spot for gay men.

The murderer used Sigler's keys to steal his 1994 white Toyota Celica, which bore Texas license plates. The car was still missing.

Investigators believed the date of the murder was significant because it helped them pinpoint exactly when Cunanan arrived in South Florida.

"We're definitely looking at this as being related to the Versace murder," one police source told Miami reporters.

There was even talk from Manila of Cunanan being the suspect in the unsolved murder of gay fashion designer Carlos Badidoy. But investigators failed to confirm if Cunanan was even in the Philippines at the time of the killing.

But as Cunanan's name became linked to more and more crimes, he remained as elusive as ever.

In Miami, families kept their children off the streets and gun dealers reported a rush of sales from worried residents. Police were swamped with calls from frightened locals urging them to step up the manhunt.

There were demands for the four hundred FBI agents and police hunting Cunanan to be reinforced.

Miami police lieutenant Dale Barsness warned: "He's not your run-of-the-mill spree or serial killer. He's very intelligent, very cunning, a conman."

Attendance at gay bars and clubs on South Beach dropped dramatically in the days following Versace's killing.

Danilo de la Torre, an actor who performs as a drag queen in South Beach clubs, played to a virtually empty premises for the first time in his ten-year career.

In Washington, Attorney General Janet Reno said the FBI was doing everything it could to catch Cunanan and pledged to "make sure that we leave no stone unturned."

By shooting dead a famous personality, Andrew Cunanan had turned himself into an even more famous person than his latest victim.

Nineteen

CELEBRITY BULLETIN

Less than forty-eight hours after Versace's murder, FBI and police investigators issued a chilling warning to dozens more celebrities to be on their guard for Andrew Cunanan.

Elton John, owner of a home in Atlanta, Georgia, and a close friend of the Italian designer, was among those urged to take special care as long as Cunanan remained on the run.

John Travolta, British actor Rupert Everett, artist David Hockney, and designers Giorgio Armani, Calvin Klein, and Jean-Paul Gaultier were also alerted by authorities.

The FBI refused to publicly say what had prompted the new warning but they had been talking to some of Cunanan's friends in San Diego.

Investigators also believed that Cunanan was carrying with him that photograph taken at a party with *Friends* star Lisa Kudrow, who had irritated him by showing no interest in his acting ambitions when they met at a party almost a year earlier. She was also warned to be take extra security precautions.

On Thursday, July 17, at the specific request of the Versace family, Dade State Attorney Katherine Fernandez Rundle visited the late designer's sister Donatella and brother Santos at the Versace home on South Beach to brief them about the criminal justice process in Florida.

And more reported sightings of Cunanan flooded the FBI and Miami police. Several of the callers claimed Cunanan had been seen in the South Beach area since the Versace murder.

FBI spokeswoman Anne Figueiras said: "We've had a voluminous number of calls that have been very fruitful. Our main mission is to locate Cunanan and that's our only focus at this time."

Over at Miami police headquarters, the hunt for Cunanan took another important turn when police sniffer dogs checking out dead Cuban doctor Silvio Alfonso's black BMW recognized the scent they picked up on clothes left by Cunanan near Versace's mansion.

It now definitely looked as if Cunanan had claimed a sixth victim.

And the hunt for Andrew Cunanan had already reached cyberspace.

The New York–based Gay and Lesbian Anti-Violence Project began using the Internet to flood America with information on Cunanan within hours of the death of Gianni Versace. They even put up a $10,000 award for his capture, which was quickly matched by New York City Mayor Rudolph Giuliani.

Under a headline that read GAY ANTI-VIOLENCE GROUP POSTS CUNANAN REWARD they informed Net watchers of the grisly record of slayings to date.

The press release started:

July 16, 1997, New York City—Today, the National Coalition of Anti-Violence Programs (NCAVP) renewed its call for the Federal Bureau of Investigation (FBI) and local law enforcement agencies to work cooperatively with members of the gay, lesbian, bisexual, and transgender (GLBT) communities to apprehend suspected spree killer Andrew Cunanan.

It then went on to give detailed descriptions, photographs, accounts of his habits and interests, as well as warnings to gay men to avoid dangerous situations.

Chris Quinn, spokeswoman for the group, explained: "We're using the Net to spread the word about him. We have blanketed the country with details."

The same group also helped plaster the walls of New York's gay bars and gathering places with posters of Cunanan's face. The group believed that he had visited New York under the alias of Andy DeSilva during the previous six months.

Generally, the Internet was buzzing as gay groups and individuals exchanged information, fears, and safety tips from each other across the country.

The FBI's Ten Most Wanted List website took an estimated 20,000 "hits" during the Thursday after Versace's death as Net-surfers—both the curious and the frightened—visited the site to read about suspect Cunanan.

The site featured a selection of photos of Cunanan. Some even downloaded them and had them printed and distributed. Such prints were being handed out at entrances to gay bars across the city as grave-faced bouncers urged visitors to "take care now."

Also on the Internet, a number of Gianni Versace sites had mushroomed since the designer's death. They included Internet obituaries, sentimental tributes, pictures of models wearing his fashions, photographs of Versace, as well as newspaper reports.

Some police forces across the country even issued warnings to Internet users about the danger that lurked in "Internet liaisons." There were genuine fears that Cunanan might try to make contact with an intended next victim through the Internet.

A police spokesman in New York warned: "We caution people to take the utmost care. There can be no guarantee of safety in such encounters. Now, above all, is the time for prudence. You never know who you'll find at the end of an Internet invitation.''

Back in Miami Beach there was continual fallout from the murder of Gianni Versace. Everyone on South Beach was being especially careful; sales clerks were scrutinizing customers' faces trying to catch a resemblance to Cunanan.

Others were worried about their own personal safety when they strolled on the sidewalk or in the dozens of gay bars and clubs near the Versace mansion. Many had given up walking or cycling at night and were taking taxis instead.

Despite the police and FBI warnings that Cunanan could still be in the vicinity of South Beach, some gay men in the city still felt an overwhelming sense of loss rather than any new sense of fear.

Ironically, it had been the area's easygoing atmosphere that had attracted Gianni Versace in the first place. Now this social playground—one of the nation's top vacation destinations for gays and a focus of the party scene—had been tainted with a violent, cold-blooded, high-profile murder.

Miami Beach police also enlisted the help of several influential gay men to help them track down Cunanan. They feared that many of the city's gay population would be frightened to come forward with important clues about Cunanan's movements during the period he spent in Miami before Versace's death.

''It's like a sick feeling in the city,'' explained Bob Gilmartin, vice-president of the Florida Hotel Network, a hotel reservation company representing most of the hotels on South Beach. ''Everyone's thinking that this sense of innocence we have here is going to be taken away by this tragic act.''

Meanwhile others were bitter that there hadn't been more

publicity about Cunanan's killing spree *before* he claimed victim number five, Gianni Versace.

"I want to know why we weren't warned, "said Glenn Albin, the editor-in-chief of *Ocean Drive* magazine, a local monthly.

Albin was infuriated because he'd seen posters all over Greenwich Village when he'd visited New York in May while there were virtually none in Miami. "This is like a lifeguard seeing sharks coming and waiting for somebody to go down," added Albin.

It wasn't until two days after Versace's death that South Beach businesses like Idols Gym and the West End Bar finally began displaying posters the police gave them on the night after Versace's killing.

However, other gay residents in South Beach were relieved that Versace appeared to have been targeted and was not the victim of a random killing. They believed that such an act would have ruined the comfort level in the area, where gay people could walk hand-in-hand at all times of the day and night.

And the tributes continued to pour in. At one of Versace's favorite nightclubs, The Warsaw, bar manager Taylor Boyd, thirty, said: "We all loved him. He didn't live on the island all isolated like the other celebrities. He said, 'This is my home, those are my people, this is where I want to be.'"

In a remarkably swift move, the Dade County Medical Examiner released Versace's body to his family within two days of the designer's murder. He was cremated almost immediately and a memorial mass was held in Miami the following day at St. Patrick's Roman Catholic Church.

Inevitably, comparisons were drawn to the death of John Lennon in New York City in 1980.

Gary Knight, a managed-care director in South Beach, who headed the community relations board, said: "We've certainly lost an individual who contributed to making South

Beach an international destination. But I don't think New York City was changed when John Lennon was killed and I don't expect South Beach to change because of this.''

Reported sightings of Cunanan in South Beach bars prompted yet another tour of all gay establishments by Miami police officers and FBI agents armed with photographs of the suspect. They particularly concentrated on amorous couples and gay men who admitted a fondness for casual sex.

Police then stumbled upon evidence that Cunanan staked out the Versace mansion for many weeks before he shot the fashion designer. Staff at the 11th Street Diner just two blocks from the Versace mansion recognized photos of Cunanan and said he would often sit in the diner for hours at time drinking one cup of coffee and studying the area in the direction of Versace's home.

Two days after the Versace murder, Cunanan's mother was tracked down by journalists at her small condo in San Diego. She revealed that she'd told FBI investigators how her husband had abandoned his family and she now existed solely on food stamps as a means of support.

MaryAnn Cunanan, under round-the-clock police guard, also insisted that she could not believe that her son was responsible for at least five violent deaths.

"No matter what he's done, he's my flesh and blood. I can't believe he could be a cold-blooded killer.''

She then added: "I just hope he's not the next one.''

But by the next day she seemed to have become more resigned to her son's murderous activities.

FBI agents who revisited her said she now believed her son had "snapped'' after learning that he was HIV-positive.

"I feel he has done these things as an act of revenge,'' MaryAnn Cunanan said.

She added: "He used to be such a good child. He learned

to read the Bible before he was six years old from cover to cover, and he had read every word in an encyclopedia by the age of fourteen. But then as he grew older I noticed he became more effeminate and we had some serious differences."

She once again repeated that her son was a male prostitute. She made it sound as if it was just one of those things.

The high-profile nature of the case following Versace's killing had an unfortunate effect for the families of Cunanan's other alleged victims. The worldwide notoriety thrust their pain and anguish back into the spotlight just when some of them were starting to try and rebuild their lives.

Property developer Lee Miglin's wife Marilyn wasn't surprised when she heard that the man suspected of killing her husband had murdered once again.

A feeling of profound sadness, kept at bay in the preceding few weeks only by keeping busy with work, descended on her once more as she bowed her head and thought: "Another family has been torn apart and now must go through the heartbreak."

Marilyn Miglin was convinced that the massive press coverage would wet Cunanan's appetite to commit more murders.

"He is a foxy, crafty fellow," she said. "And he clearly has a sick desire to be the center of attention."

Marilyn Miglin, owner of a cosmetics company, did not personally know Gianni Versace, but she did know the manager of the Versace boutique in Chicago.

She even called her friend immediately and told her: "I know what you are about to experience and can empathize with your nightmare as we have been through it."

For weeks after her own husband's brutal murder Marilyn Miglin woke up most mornings and thought that what had happened was just a bad dream. Then she would look over and realize her husband was no longer there.

Her two children Marlena Miglin Craig and Duke Miglin helped her get through the day but it was very difficult.

"Lee and I lived each day to the fullest," said Marilyn, close to tears. "We enjoyed life and each other."

Victim Jeffrey Trail's mother Ann broke down when she heard that Cunanan's name was being linked to the Versace slaying.

"It's a hard loss when it's something so violent and unnecessary," she said at the family home in DeKalb, Illinois. "He's destroyed an awful lot of lives. Maybe this will be his last."

It was during a visit to Chicago's O'Hare International Airport the week before Versace's killing that Ann Trail realized how Cunanan continued to avoid capture.

"With all the activity and people at the airport . . . he could have been standing within three feet of me and I wouldn't know it," she said. "He certainly has fooled everybody. But his capture won't bring Jeffrey back."

Trail's father Stan was so shaken by the resurgence of interest in his son's death that he sent a letter to his local newspaper.

"I don't really need this," he said. "In my heart I know that in his final hour he was kind honorable, honest, audacious, sympathetic, caring, and strong."

Also in the Midwest, the Madson family were once more facing reminders of their loved one's death.

Madson's brother Ralph Madson said word of the Versace slaying arrived at a bad moment for the family because relatives were going through the dead man's belongings.

"We just hope they get him," said Madson. "This is another tragedy. The killing has to stop . . . This person is an animal."

Throughout the Twin Cities, home of Cunanan's first two

victims, chilling shock waves were felt after the Versace killing.

News of Versace's death created a buzz of fear in the Warehouse district where David Madson had lived until his death.

Chris Paddock, owner of Bobino Cafe and Wine Bar recalled how several of his employees raced into work on the day of Versace's death and asked him if he was aware of the fashion designer's death.

"He's an icon for many in the gay community," said Paddock.

Local resident Keith Lee, who had attended a Versace birthday party in Miami Beach only a few weeks previously, said: "I don't think the gay factor in regards to Cunanan is a factor at all. I think people just look at him as another psycho killer. People are more open-minded now."

Dave King, owner of Caffe Solo, also in Minneapolis, had Cunanan pegged as the suspect in the Versace killing two hours before it was publicly announced. His restaurant was across the street from Madson's Harmony Loft Apartments home.

King even remembered Cunanan and Madson visiting the Caffe Solo just before his death. He said it was "kind of creepy" how a tragic, isolated incident so close to his business had now turned into international news.

Disturbingly, the publicity surrounding the killing had forced the owners of Harmony Loft to take down its outdoor sign because of homophobic attacks by passing youths.

On the evening of Thursday, July 17, San Diego AIDS counselor Mike Dudley finally plucked up enough courage to call the FBI and tell them about his out-of-control meeting with Cunanan the previous January.

When he told investigators the full story of how Cunanan had flipped out and appeared to have been told he had AIDS, the Bureau considered it even further evidence that their killer on-the-run was HIV-positive—and that made him even more reckless and dangerous to the general public.

Dudley's boss at David's Place clinic, Karen Moreland, insisted the counselor took so long to call investigators because he hadn't wanted to break confidences.

"Normally we don't break confidences, but if you think you have information that can help in a crime, I feel morally you have to say something," said Karen Moreland.

Frank Sabatini, a gay and lesbian group organizer in San Diego was convinced Cunanan was HIV-positive.

"He very well could have been predisposed and this might have pushed him over the edge. This was the first thing that makes a smidgen of sense. The people I've known who've been HIV-positive have been thrown into a depressive state or become very spiritual. It's a real metamorphosis—although I've never seen anyone become violent before."

The FBI, now with more than four hundred agents hunting Cunanan, still hadn't solved the biggest mystery of all: why had he killed all these people?

"What would motivate him?" asked Special Agent Carl Chamber of the FBI's San Diego office. "That's the $64,000 question. We have no clues."

As for his location, the FBI remained convinced Cunanan was still in South Florida.

"We're going to assume he's in South Florida until we have a credible sighting of him in another location," said FBI spokeswoman Anne Figueiras.

Twenty

COMEDY OF ERRORS

It wasn't until Friday July 18—three days after Versace's death—that the FBI finally established that Cunanan had actually been staying at the Normandy Plaza Hotel for some time before the Versace killing.

An emergency call to the hotel the day after the Versace murder drew a complete blank when the FBI was told that Cunanan was staying in the wrong room. It was yet another example of the federal agents' "bad luck." Others would call it sloppy investigating work.

This time police immediately crowded into the hotel on Collins Avenue, Miami Beach's main drag, after the manager recontacted them to say he'd located the rooms where Cunanan had definitely stayed.

Staff told investigators that Cunanan skipped out of the hotel shortly before the Versace killing without paying the previous night's rent.

All he left behind was a pile of fashion magazines, hair clippers, and an electric razor—items that the staff threw out before realizing the notoriety of their missing guest.

This time police evacuated guests and searched all sixty-five rooms in case Cunanan was still in the building. But he had long since departed.

By the weekend, South Florida was still awash with reported sightings of Cunanan, but absolutely nothing concrete materialized. The alleged murderer of Gianni Versace had been "seen" in bars, in discos, in Key West.

Even a sex shop manager near Versace's vast villa told police of a well-dressed, well-spoken regular customer resembling Cunanan who bought some sex toys.

In the Lake Worth area, just south of West Palm Beach, a barman named Gannon Woekel insisted that Cunanan had drunk at his tavern. Woekel said he was too terrified to call the police until the man had gone. The police took a Heineken beer bottle drunk by "Cunanan" away for fingerprint testing.

They'd already discovered that the prints they lifted from Bill Reese's red Chevy pickup were too smudged to be recognizable. All they had was a thumbprint from Cunanan's pawn shop receipt.

Even a *Miami Herald* newspaper reporter, Johnny Diaz, was briefly "identified" as Cunanan after a source he was interviewing decided he looked just like the serial killer. The interviewee called the FBI, who questioned Diaz.

The alleged sightings of Cunanan fitted in with the theory that he was still playing a cat-and-mouse game with police and FBI agents, teasing them with a deliberate trail of clues following his rampage of killings, which many believed would eventually number more than five.

Investigators remained convinced that Cunanan left one of his passports in Bill Reese's red Chevy pickup and another in Lee Miglin's Lexus as part of a deliberate plan to keep police warm on his trail.

After all, he could just as easily have fled the Versace killing in the pickup. Instead he chose to disappear by foot and possibly taxi. Investigators even believed he deliberately left some of his blood-stained clothes near the vehicle to attract police to it.

But federal authorities also feared that all these "clues"

and "calling cards" indicated that Cunanan might be planning a major coup—either another celebrity killing, or staging his own death in a final shoot-out with police—and he did not intend to try and flee the country, though he was believed to still have a forged French passport.

FBI agents also became convinced that Cunanan had returned to the murder scene hours after Versace's death to gloat at what he had done and watch the investigators.

A man closely resembling Cunanan was actually filmed by a video security camera above Versace's gate in the throng of people that gathered around the blood-stained steps of the fashion designer's house on Ocean Drive.

The FBI examined all the footage it could obtain of the spectators, Versace's friends and associates, and the many strangers who placed flowers on the steps and lit candles.

The scene had been chaoticly similar to the outpouring of grief around the Dakota Building in New York following the shooting of John Lennon. It was very simple for the wanted man to stand unnoticed in the crowd.

Criminologists had long since warned the FBI that Cunanan had the classic "ordinary" features that would enable him to fit in anywhere.

Jack Levin, a criminologist at Northeastern University in Boston, said: "He's Mr. America. He looks like everybody, yet he looks like no one in particular. I really don't think he's a master of disguise. He's extraordinarily ordinary."

FBI agents even blew up sections of the video footage and transmitted them to their offices in San Diego where agents showed them to friends of Cunanan. Within hours they had confirmed it was indeed him standing outside the Versace mansion hours after the killing.

In San Diego, the man who took the last recorded photograph of Cunanan back on March 9 in a Hillcrest gay club was living in fear that Cunanan might be after him.

"I had forgotten about the pictures until after Versace's murder. When I saw who the police were after, it rang a bell. I checked my snaps and there he was. I am now terrified he will come after me. I am releasing them in the hope they might help capture him. I just hope the cops find him soon so I can rest easy in my bed at night."

In the world of fashion, many designers were genuinely fearful that Cunanan might make them his next target.

In New York, Calvin Klein exited a Manhattan menswear display via a loading bay in which his black Mercedes was parked, engine running. As it shot off, three security men ran alongside it Secret Service-style.

Then the FBI issued a bizarre warning that Cunanan might still be in the Miami area—dressed as a woman. They even issued a picture showing what Cunanan might look like dressed in drag.

With this latest warning, the permutations for alleged sightings of him became almost endless.

In Fort Lauderdale, someone reported spotting Cunanan in a peach dress in a Publix supermarket, pushing his cart along the narrow aisles, eyeing produce and cereal boxes.

Then his male alter ego was alleged to have been seen sipping a beer at Gator Kick, a South Dade County strip club. A slew of other people reported him either hanging back or carousing at just about every gay bar within driving distance of South Miami Beach.

In a suburban section of Miami one person claimed they'd seen Cunanan milling about the neighborhood in a gray skirt, white top, and gray wig.

The sightings transcended state borders. Police received more calls from New York, Mississippi, South Carolina, and New Mexico. One caller claimed that Cunanan had been seen in a field of okra in Arkansas.

Many of the sightings defied logic. Sergeant John Roper

coordinator for Crime Stoppers in Dade County, which answered telephone tips, summed it up: "It's not quite as bad as Elvis. At least we know this guy is alive."

On Friday, July 18, the requiem mass for Gianni Versace at St. Patrick's Catholic Church was a strange affair by anyone's standards.

It was part holy rite, part kitsch, part wake for Versace's adopted family—the gays and beautiful people of Miami Beach. And a noisy summer thunderstorm raged overhead.

St. Patrick's—a mock Renaissance church with a mock Romanesque campanile—was airy, built of pale stone with graceful arches and a reasonably well-crafted rose window. There were plans to renovate it—as a divine reflection of the revival of the hedonist Miami Beach days of the Roaring Twenties—with gold-leaf finishes.

It was what Miami residents call an old building, erected in 1926. Al Capone used to come here to pray for his soul.

But men with guns were the invisible enemy this time as seven hundred people arrived from all over America. Some—the bronzed and beautiful—wore Versace clothes. Others wore T-shirts, shorts, and sneakers. Some wore black, others denim.

The expected celebrities like Sly Stallone and Madonna stayed away, as did Versace's family, who sent a message of appreciation through a spokesman.

But these were not the visitors sought by one of the biggest contingents present: the hundreds of uniformed police officers who surrounded the church and the plainclothes-but-barely-disguised FBI agents who mingled in the crowd.

Convinced that Cunanan might make an appearance at Versace's memorial, agents walked up and down the aisles of the church throughout the ceremony. They inspected the faces of every dignitary, businessman, model, and fashion industry consultant and scanned the crowds listening to the ceremony by loudspeaker outside the church.

At one stage one of the mourners told agents she thought she'd seen Cunanan in the church. But it turned out to be a newspaper reporter.

Outside the church, police handed out pictures of Cunanan just to make sure that if anyone recognized the suspected killer he would be immediately apprehended.

Inside, Father Patrick O'Neill told the mourners: "Gianni will be clothing everyone in outrageous outfits in Heaven."

After days of fevered speculation that Cunanan had struck again in the death of Cuban doctor Silvio Alfonso, the Florida Department of Law Enforcement announced the two murders were "definitely not connected."

Metro Dade Police Sergeant Pete Andreu told reporters: "At this time we have no substantial lead linking Andrew Cunanan to this investigation other than a witness describing similar physical characteristics. This could well be a wild goose chase. But with the subject having a close resemblance, we had to pursue every avenue we had."

Meanwhile federal and local investigators widened their net to check out the murders of all homosexual males along the entire east coast of the country since early May when Cunanan began heading south following the murder of Bill Reese.

The FBI remained convinced Cunanan was feeding his ego by remaining in South Florida to watch the nonstop media coverage of the nationwide manhunt.

And yet more theories abounded to explain Cunanan's killing spree.

Investigators now believed that Cunanan—whom they said was definitely HIV-positive—was targeting people he was convinced had infected or humiliated him.

"The trauma is clear-cut," explained Dr. Allen Scott, a

psychologist with the Miami police. "And now, because of his predisposition to killing, it works into his fantasies. Perhaps as his final attention-getting gesture he is saving the best for last. He clearly wanted to be associated with the Versace murder."

In Miami, police were still trying desperately to locate one of the four cars stolen within a few hours of the Versace killing from locations near the parking lot where Bill Reese's red Chevy pickup was found.

A black Nissan Pathfinder was driven away by a man resembling Cunanan. But the trail had gone cold immediately after the car disappeared.

Detectives even took the unusual step of allowing TV stations to show videotape of the figure wearing shorts and a T-shirt—presumably Cunanan—running down an alley minutes after the Versace murder.

However, investigators admitted that at least half of the video cameras operating near Versace's house and on the escape route taken by Cunanan had not been functioning correctly and many of the available tapes were of poor quality.

The slaying of Gianni Versace was at least having one positive effect; it helped strengthen the cases against Cunanan in connection with all the other murders he was suspected of committing.

Faith Hochberg, the United States Attorney in Newark, New Jersey, announced that Cunanan was being officially charged with the May 9 murder of cemetery caretaker Bill Reese. This was a significant move by authorities as these were the first federal murder charges to be filed against Andrew Cunanan.

These charges were brought about because of the evidence found inside Reese's truck when it was discovered near the home of Gianni Versace.

Chicago County Attorney Jim Reuter, whose area covered

the location of the David Madson slaying, said it was unclear which jurisdiction would be the first to prosecute. That would depend on which one had the best case.

But he admitted that investigators had established definite evidence linking the bullets that killed Madson with the gun being used by Cunanan.

"It appears that each tragedy this man is involved in strengthens the case we have. I'm just hoping he will be captured in Miami," explained Reuter.

But investigators were still lacking one of the most important clues in any murder inquiry—a clear set of fingerprints or any other type of identifying features.

Investigators even went back to forensic experts with the half-eaten ham sandwich they found in Lee Miglin's home following his slaying in the hopes of cross-checking the teeth marks with Cunanan's dental records. But still there was no sign of any dental records and, in any case, forensics warned that the teeth marks were not very clear.

Investigators continued to come up with new composites of how Cunanan might have changed his hair, grown a beard, or shaved his head. They also returned to San Diego, San Francisco and Minnesota to reinterview his numerous friends and acquaintances in those cities.

Authorities even sent notices to 150 countries across the world to check passport details of any arriving passengers in case Cunanan had managed to get out of the country.

As the hours turned into days following the murder of Gianni Versace, it became clear that Andrew Cunanan would not be as easily apprehended as many had presumed when he darted into the crowd following his last slaying.

Across America people were starting to ask why had he not been caught. There was a backlash against the rubberneckers and thrill-seekers who were talking about Cunanan as if he were some sort of criminal hero.

As *OutNOW!* A gay publication pointed out in an editorial following Versace's death:

> The person who bludgeoned Jeffrey Trail to death is no hero. Neither is the person who repeatedly shot David Madson, who tortured and slashed Lee Miglin, who coldly murdered William Reese, and who twice shot Gianni Versace in the back of the head before walking calmly away.
>
> If Andrew Cunanan imagines himself to be in a catch-me-if-you-can game, it's one he alone has the leisure to play. For law enforcement officers, and for society, the pursuit of Cunanan has become ever-more urgent. After five brutal killings, it's not just a question of catching the man who did it. It's even more a question of catching him before he does it again.

The ashes of Gianni Versace were flown back to Italy on Friday, July 18.

The designer's brother Santo and sister Donatella arrived from Miami Beach on a Challenger 600 private jet at a small airport near Bergamo, in northern Italy, shortly before five P.M.

Then Santo and Donatella boarded an Augusta 109 helicopter to fly to the shores of Lake Como. Within thirty minutes of landing on Italian soil, the late designer's ashes were speeding through the gates of the family's lakeside retreat in a Mercedes. Donatella was clutching a bouquet of flowers.

The Villa Fontanelle stood near the village of Moltrasio at the southern end of the lake. Parish priest Father Bartolomeo Franzi told reporters he had been asked by family representatives to make himself available to bless the ashes in a service to be held in the local cemetery that evening.

A strong police presence and teams of security guards sealed off the villa and the cemetery to ensure the service was strictly private.

A dozen mourners gathered at the cemetery overlooking the Italian village of Moltrasio, overlooking Lake Como—the place where Andrew Cunanan boasted he had first met Versace.

Priest Bartolomeo Franzi told the family: "May the Lord help us to understand what has befallen you."

The ashes were then left, temporarily, in a simple burial niche.

The plan was to transport them to Milan for a memorial mass on the following Tuesday. After that they would be buried in the grounds of the villa.

On Sunday, July 20—six days after the Versace killing—the FBI escalated its efforts to find Cunanan, activating a central command facility in Washington used during another top-priority case of domestic horror: the Oklahoma bombing in 1995.

Twice daily, agents in five cities—Minneapolis, Miami, Chicago, Philadelphia, and San Diego—conferred by conference telephone calls to access progress in what had become the biggest manhunt in U.S. history. They fully intended to continue the procedure until Cunanan was run to ground.

Authorities remained convinced that Cunanan was still in South Florida, possibly trying to meld anonymously into a gay community outside Miami or hunkering down in a "safe house" or perhaps sleeping in a stolen car.

A nationwide bulletin had gone out to officers who patrolled the country's freeways.

The warning raised the frightening specter for law enforcement that Cunanan could be capable of yet another kind of killing: killing to avoid capture, the last desperate act of a fugitive.

"I'm worried about that patrol officer in Wyoming who might stop Cunanan's car without knowing who he is and what he's capable of," fugitive task force coordinator Bill Sorukas explained to reporters covering the story.

"I'm praying we get that one phone call that tells us where he is."

In San Diego's Hillcrest district, Cunanan was the subject on most people's minds. There was real concern among his friends and associates that he might return to his hometown with murder on his mind.

Police genuinely feared that Cunanan might turn up at the soon-to-be-held Lesbian and Gay Pride Parade, expected to attract 85,000 people.

After all, Cunanan had actually been an active member of the gay coalition in San Diego that encouraged gays to practice safe sex. Those gay men that Cunanan once tried to help were now very afraid of him and many were expected to stay away from the parade.

Many of the participants and spectators at the show, a tradition for twenty-two years, would be wearing costumes and theatrical makeup, which would make it easy for Cunanan to return in disguise.

"He could be walking in the crowd and nobody would know it," said San Diego Police Lieutenant Jim Collins. "That's what we have to contend with."

Back in Miami Beach, police were now having to contend with the fact that their manhunt was a womanhunt as well.

"Not only do we have to look for someone who looks like everybody, we have to look for someone who looks like everybody, dressed as a girl," said one weary investigator.

In San Diego, one of Cunanan's oldest friends got a nasty shock one afternoon—six days after Gianni Versace's death—when he played back his answerphone.

"Hi, it's Andy. The FBI will never catch me—I'm just too damn clever."

The call was from a public phone somewhere in Miami.

Twenty-one

THE DRAG ARTIST

Outside the Versace headquarters on Via Gesu, in Milan, Italy, a simple wreath of yellow flowers hung on the vast wooden door with a small white card beside it.

It read MOURNING FOR THE DEATH OF GIANNI VERSACE, TUESDAY, JULY 22, 1997, 1800 LOCAL TIME, A REMEMBRANCE MASS WILL BE HELD IN THE CATHEDRAL OF MILAN.

Just a mile away, inside the magnificent Duomo, Milan's fourteenth-century cathedral, the tiny casket containing the ashes of Gianni Versace sat on the middle of a lace-covered table.

To the right was a gold-framed photo of a bare-chested Versace. To the left lay his book, a eulogy of prose and photos entitled *Do Not Disturb*.

Further to the left and the right of the table were ornate gold and malachite candelabra supported by gold cherubs holding aloft seven candles.

Toward the front were silver vases holding white, sweet-smelling freesias and roses, Versace's favorite flowers.

Yellow drapes darkened the room.

There seems little doubt that wherever Andrew Cunanan was on that Tuesday, July 22, he must have seen TV footage of the extraordinary turnout at the memorial mass for his most famous victim.

It was by all accounts, a remarkable public showing of grief by some of the most famous people in the world.

Princess Diana comforted a weeping Elton John for forty-five minutes as the heartbroken singer sobbed quietly beside the princess at the mass in Milan's picturesque Roman Catholic Cathedral.

Diana, wearing Versace black, even leaned across to pat Elton's arm gently and whisper condolences.

Versace's family and friends had been joined by the celebrity-studded mourners who packed into the ancient Gothic cathedral in tribute to the Italian fashion guru.

Elton John was already overcome with emotion from an earlier visit to the Versace mansion in Milan where the designer's ashes were displayed in their golden casket.

At one stage during the church service, Elton John took off his diamond-shaped glasses and wiped his eyes with a white handkerchief.

Then he held his head in his hands.

He then composed himself sufficiently to perform, with Versace's other close showbusiness friend, rock star Sting, the Twenty-third Psalm, "The Lord is My Shepherd."

Dotted around the church were books of dedication for people to sign. Many did with tears streaming down their cheeks.

In his address to the star-studded congregation Monsignor Angelo Majo said: "We are not here to put on a show but to mourn the loss of a friend, a brother in the eyes of God.

"A man who spreads goodness throughout his life is not afraid of death. Death is a sign of hope.

"We are here because our Gianni was called to the other side, proof we are all equal human beings in the eyes of God.

"The soul of the righteous is eternal. We are here to remember and commemorate Gianni Versace, snatched from life by an unexpected tragedy. Contemporary society unfortunately does not know how to deal with death.

"We are here to share the pain with Gianni's brother Santos and his sister Donatella so that they do not feel alone when they carry on the work of their brother."

An hour earlier, Princess Diana had flown to Milan by private jet and gone straight to Versace's Milan villa to pay her respects at twelve minutes to five.

As she stepped through the front door she was greeted by Versace's heartbroken sister Donatella. They kissed.

The princess then spent several minutes alone in the room that held the ashes.

She was then taken to another room where she changed into a new Versace dress for the memorial service.

Other guests at the memorial service included Naomi Campbell, who had to be supported as she emerged from a Mercedes limousine outside the cathedral.

There were other VIPs including Carolyn Bessette, wife of John Kennedy Junior, designers Giorgio Armani, Gianfranco Ferre, Valentino, and Karl Lagerfeld.

In the front row was Versace's longtime live-in lover Antonio d'Amico.

Male mourners virtually all wore dark suits, dark ties and white shirts while women came in black jackets and trousers or simple black dresses.

More than twenty police officers guarded the entrance, and steel rails were put up on the pavements outside to keep bystanders at a distance as friends and family came and went in the summer sunshine.

Others far removed from Versace's glamorous world of celebrities also arrived at the cathedral to pay their last respects.

More than one hundred workers from a Versace factory outside Milan travelled by bus to attend the mass.

Inside the cathedral, a Versace aide said proudly: "Gianni liked things kept simple. He loved beautiful people and beautiful flowers, particularly white roses."

The huge turnout at the cathedral was a true measure of Versace's immense popularity. It was also a measure of the fame which probably cost him his life.

After the service, the family held a small reception for close friends at the Versace headquarters on Via Gesu.

The street was closed, with the carabinieri on patrol, but hundreds of onlookers crowded the sidewalk, many carrying bunches of flowers.

Later, Versace's ashes were taken back to his villa on Lake Como, where they were to be scattered in a private ceremony.

The memorial mass was supposed to bring home the religious significance of Gianni Versace's violent death. But with the crowds surging at the doors and the congregation stuffed with the most unlikely churchgoers, it was only a brief moment of reflection before the cameras started rolling all over again.

On the same day as Versace's memorial mass in Milan, police in Miami admitted they were no closer to catching Cunanan. They still believed he was disguised in drag much of the time and was probably within a few miles of the site of his last confirmed killing, that of Gianni Versace.

Meanwhile, private security consultant Frank Monte who had been working for Gianni Versace to help uncover the Mafia infiltration of his fashion business, was helping FBI officials with their investigation into the designer's death.

Eight days after Versace's death, Monte told investigators: "As far as I am concerned, this was a professional hit ordered by organized criminals. If I could contact Cunanan I would tell him to call me because I think he's innocent."

Police had initially called Monte after finding some of his company brochures and reports inside the Versace mansion in South Beach. But at first they failed to follow up because they were so convinced that Cunanan had acted entirely alone in killing Versace.

But it was a measure of how few leads they now had that they felt desperate enough to contact Monte. The Mob hit theory was gaining credibility the longer Cunanan remained at liberty.

In New York, rumors began spreading that Cunanan was heading for the city.

Howard Safir, the city's police commissioner, sought to douse the panic by doubling the presence of uniformed officers in the gay quarters of Chelsea and Greenwich Village.

New York had been high on the list of potential hideouts for Cunanan, ever since that entry was discovered in his diary as investigators searched his San Diego home in early May following the murder of David Madson, his second victim.

Cunanan wrote: "If I need to get lost, it's going to be in New York."

The words, widely publicized throughout the city, chilled New York's thriving gay scene.

Some were saying that Cunanan had been "the worst thing to happen to America's gays since AIDS started."

And Cunanan's name was completely wiped clear of the list of suspects in the murder of Cuban doctor Silvio Alfonso after police arrested a man for the slaying.

"An arrest has been made," said a Miami police spokesman. "The subject arrested is not Andrew Cunanan."

The subject was in fact another Cuban called Yosvani Fernandez who bore a passing resemblance to Cunanan and had decided to kill Alfonso in an argument about money.

Undoubtedly the confusion caused by this unconnected killing had given Andrew Cunanan even more space to survive.

Twenty-two

BLANK CHECK

By the morning of Wednesday July 23—more than a week after the murder of Gianni Versace—FBI agents were forced to admit: "We have no idea where Andrew Cunanan is. He could be anywhere in the world."

They were having to face up to the likelihood that Cunanan had slipped through the net of the biggest manhunt in American criminal history.

The Bureau was coming under increasing criticism for its handling of the operation.

Many were asking why if Cunanan was already on the FBI's Ten Most Wanted List before Versace's killing didn't the manhunt properly get underway until *after* the fashion designer was murdered.

Critics wanted the answers to four vital questions and claimed that Versace would still be alive if the FBI had not blundered.

1) Why didn't the FBI and police act on information given to them that Cunanan had used his own name and provided a thumbprint in a pawn shop six days before killing Versace?

2) Why did they not spot the red Chevy pickup truck—stolen from his fourth murder victim—when it was left in

that public parking area in South Beach, Miami for at least
month, despite a so-called nationwide alert?

3) Why did they not properly warn Miami's large gay
community that Cunanan could be in their midst when they
had several confirmed sightings in late June, before Versace's murder?

4) How did the FBI manage to raid the Normandy Plaza
Hotel within hours of Versace's death and not find any trace
of Cunanan until they were called back to the same hotel
two days later?

Despite the huge public response, the fact remained that
Cunanan had stayed one step ahead of the FBI since starting
his killing spree almost three months earlier.

Not even his trail of "calling cards" had helped investigators close the net.

The FBI admitted they were reduced to relying on the
public to help their search for the serial killer.

FBI spokesperson Julie Miller even conceded: "We have
no idea where Cunanan is. There has been no development
in the investigation. We would appeal to all members of the
public to be vigilant and call us if they know where Cunanan
is."

FBI agents could not even agree among themselves what
had happened to the country's most wanted man.

Some remained convinced he was still holed up in Miami
because they could not definitely link him to any more stolen
getaway vehicles.

Others insisted that Cunanan was far too clever to hang
around after such a high-profile murder and believed he escaped within minutes of Versace's killing on July 15.

And in Miami, the gay community's initially calm response to a killer in their midst was boiling over into anger
and bitterness.

They described the initial FBI warnings before Versace's death as "pathetic."

Max Blandford, owner of the Warsaw Ballroom nightclub said: "They can get 400 cars ticketed for parking offenses, yet they can't tell us there is a serial killer in the area."

Restaurant owner Paul Galluzcio said: "Cunanan is not even being careful and the FBI can't catch him. We feel as though it really has to get serious before the FBI gets serious. To them it's like 'another faggot gets killed'—it took someone like Versace to get killed to get their full attention."

Meanwhile Andrew Cunanan had turned into what he always craved to be—the center of attention, the most wanted murderer in American history.

He was now living out the fantasy of fame that fueled his life from the time he shocked school friends with his blatantly flamboyant homosexuality.

Besides being disguised some of the time as a woman, it was presumed that Cunanan had shaved off all his distinctive thick, black hair so that when he was dressed as a man he looked different from his photos by using a wig.

His picture remained plastered on magazines, newspapers, and TV newscasts, but there had been no substantial sightings of him apart from brief stopovers.

The FBI even warned all of Cunanan's friends that they could be in danger because he might have also targeted all people he felt a grudge against.

But investigators were beginning to believe that they needed Cunanan to strike again if they were going to have any chance of capturing him.

FBI spokesman Alfred Boza made this appeal: "We need to know anything and everything. If you know that he went to breakfast every day at a particular place, we need to know that. Fear may have kept some people from calling, but we need all the help we can get."

And earlier rumors that a Brazilian woman had shot video

and photographs of Cunanan at a get-together inside the Versace mansion two days before the designer's murder were treated skeptically by investigators.

"No one has contacted us about the existence of any such videotape taken at the Versace mansion," said a Miami Beach police spokesman.

"If such a tape does exist, investigators would like the person in possession of that tape to get in touch with any of the law enforcement agencies working on the case."

Meanwhile investigators once again tried to confirm if a friendship existed between Versace and Cunanan.

Officials were looking into whether Cunanan may have been acquainted with Versace's longtime companion, Antonio d'Amico, who was also co-designer of the Versace Sport line.

And the Versace family continued to insist there was no such link.

Then one of Cunanan's longtime gay associates in San Diego contacted investigators and said that Cunanan told him he had a crush on someone in Versace's entourage, perhaps his boyfriend d'Amico. They suspected that the jealousy might have set off his violent explosion.

Police also began to believe that Versace might have been telephoned by Cunanan before he left his home to buy those newspapers and magazines at the News Cafe near his South Beach home.

They were told by friends and associates that Versace never usually went to the the News Cafe alone.

"As soon as I heard the circumstances, I immediately said to myself this was a set-up meeting," said one close friend of the designer. "You don't just walk down Ocean Drive with the idea you're going to bump into someone and kill them."

If Cunanan had contacted Versace by phone, it almost certainly would have been from a pay phone, as Cunanan never made one recorded call from his room at the Normandy Plaza Hotel.

Versace had been due to fly to Rome the day after his murder, so that fateful Tuesday may have been the only time that Cunanan could make his move.

To further fuel the rumors of a connection between the two men, a woman claimed she was at a party at the Versace mansion two days before his death and met a man who closely resembled Cunanan. But again, this was unconfirmed.

In San Diego it was revealed that among the wealthy men Cunanan had dated in the Hillcrest area was an elderly San Diego architect called Lincoln Aston. He was beaten to death with a stone obelisk in 1995.

A mentally ill drifter was found guilty of his murder in 1996 after he confessed in Colorado.

Investigators were now asking themselves if perhaps authorities had arrested the wrong man.

In Los Angeles, male model Tim Schwager realized just how lucky he was to still be alive. He was picked up by Cunanan in a West Hollywood bar earlier in the year and been almost killed by Cunanan when they went to a hotel suite together.

"Now I recall with hindsight the dangerous looks that flitted across his face when he got irritated, and how all his features would distort and cloud with anger if I criticized him," said Schwager.

Schwager, a Roman Catholic, added: "I will always believe that God watched over me that night. I pray to God, thanking him for saving me."

Back in Minneapolis, Sergeant Bob Ticich, the investigating police officer, remained convinced that Cunanan victim number two David Madson was involved in Jeff Trail's murder.

"Here's a professional who doesn't show up for work, who doesn't call anybody, and yet he's moving about of his own free will in the apartment for a few days," Ticich later explained. "It didn't appear that he was coerced."

Ticich also believed that both Madson and Cunanan may have been nearby when the manager used his passkey to open the door to Madson's apartment. For one thing, the Dalmatian had been freshly fed, watered, and walked. For another, Madson's wallet and credit cards were there.

"They intended at some point to get rid of the body," Ticich said. "They may have been surprised. It's very possible they were in close proximity when we were searching."

In Pennsville, New Jersey, the mass of worldwide publicity about Cunanan following the Versace killing was reminding residents all over again of the tragic death of caretaker Bill Reese, who lost his life only because he had a vehicle Cunanan wanted to steal.

"I think his incredible respect for life, as well as what had passed, shows how he had cared for the cemetery," Alicia Bjornson, historic preservation specialist at the adjacent Fort Mott State Park told one newspaper reporter.

"I think what I find so disturbing, as the reports keep coming out with the latest victim . . ." She stopped for a moment, stumbling as she tried to explain what it was like when the death of a private man became tangled up with the death of a celebrity and a national manhunt, when an admired friend became someone strangers refer to as "Reese, forty-five."

"To people here, he was known as Bill," says Bjornson. "I don't think anyone who lives is more important than any other."

On the Long Island Expressway, in New York City, a sharp-eyed retired police sergeant noticed what he believed to be a cross-dresser resembling Cunanan in a dark Jeep on a service road two days after Versace's death.

"The Jeep was driving erratically, I tailed it, noticed it

had Pennsylvania plates," recalled the man later.

"And suddenly this apparent cross-dresser stopped the car, got out, and feigned checking his engine. All the while he was checking me out, but not making direct eye contact."

It turned out to be yet another false lead.

At the Miami Beach sandwich shop where police missed Cunanan by a mere five minutes almost a month before Versace was murdered, employee Kenneth Benjamin was shocked to discover that the man he had tried to hand over to the police was the suspect in the killing of the Italian designer as well as the four others.

"I wanted to throw up when I found out. If only they had caught him, Versace would still be alive," said Benjamin.

One week and a day after the Versace killing, FBI Deputy Director William Esposito drew parallels between the hunt for Cunanan and the hunt for the Unabomber.

He said: "Agents are seeking out every known friend or associate of Cunanan's on the assumption he will try to contact one of them in an effort to get shelter and money."

The FBI investigation went from bad to worse when it was publicly revealed that the pawn shop receipt sent to police the day after Cunanan had been in the shop had been ignored. It had actually stated the name of the hotel where Cunanan had been staying for over a month.

The pawn shop had, as the law required, posted a copy of Cunanan's receipt to the Miami Beach Police Department, which would have arrived by July 9.

That was five days before Gianni Versace was shot in front of his South Beach home. It also happened to be more than a month after Cunanan had been put on the FBI's Ten Most Wanted List.

After days of dodging reporters, Detective Al Boza, a spokesman for Miami Beach police, responded to the revelation.

In a carefully worded press release, he explained that the

system in which the pawn shops forms were processed was not fully automated, resulting in a backlog of information.

"For that reason, there is often a time gap between the arrival of that data from the pawn shops and the entry of the information. In spite of the backlog that is created when a procedure is not automated, investigators are confident that the information would have been routed to them once it became known."

But there was no escaping the fact it was a terrible mistake that may have cost Gianni Versace his life.

Other officials in Miami were more plain-speaking about the slip-up.

"The whole purpose of the pawn shop acts is to aid the apprehension of criminals," said one official. "It is well known that criminals will take stolen goods to pawn shops, and the whole idea of making pawn shops report it is to make this possible. Obviously, Miami Beach did not have any procedures in place, and if they had, I would think they would have seen this guy was on the FBI Most Wanted List."

To add to the embarrassment of the Miami Beach Police, the Metro Dade Police Department which covers the county outside the city of Miami, would have automatically put the information into a computer on receipt of it. Officers at Metro Dade also routinely conducted another record check on a separate computer to see if the person was wanted. That meant an instant search purely by name was accessible.

Back at the pawn shop, owner Rome Riveron told reporters he was weighing up offers to sell the story to the media for at least $10,000.

Andrew Cunanan's luck was quite extraordinary.

Back on South Beach, life was slowly returning to normality.

Some people were actually enjoying the notoriety.

Local businessman Eugene Patron pointed out: "You're talking an entire economy built on dangerous sex. And the awful thing is that this killing will merely give South Beach more publicity.''

Outside Versace's mansion the prophecy seemed all too prescient. Muscle-bound boys in skimpy clothes still sailed by on their bikes and skateboards as scores of tourists gawked at the house and videotaped the scene from TV trucks.

Then, suddenly, a young man with a wad of leaflets appeared on the sidewalk and began thrusting them at everyone. They were advertisements for one of Versace's favorite nightspots.

And there were plenty of takers . . .

Twenty-three

APPOINTMENT
WITH DESTINY

Indian Creek, Miami Beach, is a canallike waterway across the street from the beach and a mass of high-rise condominiums.

At 3:58 P.M. on Wednesday, July 23, Portuguese-born caretaker Fernando Carreira was returning from his vacation with his wife when he stopped by to check over one of the vacant houseboats he guarded for German owner Torsten Reineck.

As Carreira and his wife boarded the two-story houseboat berthed at 5250 Collins Avenue, Indian Creek, he noticed that the front door was unlocked. Then he heard movement from upstairs.

Leaving his wife in the lobby, seventy-one-year-old Carreira drew his gun and went up the houseboat's spiral staircase to the second floor.

Suddenly he found himself face to face with a dark-haired man in his mid-twenties. The stranger was wearing a red bandana on his head.

The two stared at each other for a split second. The stranger looked at the gun in Carreira's hand and fled toward a bedroom.

Fernando Carreira immediately rushed back down to the lobby and grabbed his wife.

"It's him. I'm sure," he told her as he grabbed her arm and virtually dragged her out of the front door and down the ramp toward Collins Avenue.

Carreira then headed to the nearest phone to alert the police.

Inside the houseboat, Andrew Cunanan heard the caretaker rushing out onto the sidewalk.

He knew they'd be there very soon.

Cunanan walked over to the corner of the room and lay down on the floor by a walk-in closet. The end was near.

He turned Jeff Trail's Remington Peters .40 caliber gun toward himself and pushed the barrel into his mouth.

His finger brushed the trigger for a beat. Then he squeezed it hard and blew half his face away.

Moments later Fernando Carreira was on the phone to his fifteen-year-old son at home and told him: "Call the cops now. We got an intruder, and I think it's that serial killer guy."

At Miami Beach police headquarters the call was taken very seriously because there had already been two earlier reports of Cunanan in that specific vicinity.

Police cruiser radios were soon crackling with the information.

"A young white male fitting Cunanan's description ... caretaker saw an intruder ... heard at least one shot ... caretaker's OK ... we don't know if the suspect is still there."

Within minutes SWAT teams were in position across the street from the houseboat.

Protected by black flak jackets from neck to groin, carrying riot squad shields, armed with shotguns, M-16 automatic assault rifles, or stubby Uzi machine pistols, dozens of SWAT men ran across Collins Avenue, between the palm trees, and took up positions on the quay.

Some crawled on their bellies toward the ramp leading to the houseboat. Other squatted behind a red-and-white four-wheel drive parked beside the houseboat.

Within ten minutes more than one hundred FBI agents and police complete with dog teams had taken up their positions. They had sealed off busy Collins Avenue and the surrounding area—just forty blocks from Gianni Versace's South Beach mansion.

On the sundecks of surrounding high-rise apartment buildings, they trained the sights of their high-velocity rifles on the houseboat.

Police helicopters circled overhead, and official Miami Vice-style powerboats sealed off Indian Creek from any vessels, using loud hailers to warn everyone to keep away.

For more than two hours police remained happy to sit and wait. It was a classic standoff situation recorded by dozens of TV cameras and helicopter news crews hovering overhead.

Then at 7:30 P.M. a telephone and line were thrown inside the entrance to the houseboat in the hope that Cunanan might start talking to police and FBI agents now lining the entire area surrounding the boat.

"Pick up the phone, talk to us," one negotiator shouted in the direction of the houseboat.

As time wore on, the policemen looked increasingly relaxed. They firmly believed there was no one inside, not at least alive.

Just after eight, as the pink sun began disappearing from view, SWAT men fired three tear gas grenade launchers. Then five more, sending smoke up from the corner of the houseboat.

"Come out, come out now!" the lead SWAT man yelled from behind a shield with a slit for his eyes. He repeated it several times, but there was no response.

Three minutes later, the SWAT team leader moved in, up

the ramp, followed by five other officers in single file, wearing gas masks and each carrying a rifle and shield,

At 8:15 they pushed the door open and burst in. The houseboat had been shuttered, but the open door revealed that the place was, lit.

They moved around slowly, almost casually. Within minutes a policeman's walkie-talkie crackled:

"Negative on initial search," one of the SWAT team radioed back to senior officers waiting outside on the quay.

At nine, Miami police spokesman Alfred Boza announced to the waiting media: "No one is inside."

The combined forces of more than four hundred FBI and police appeared to have missed the most wanted man in America—or so it would seem.

Curious sightseers began to go home.

In fact, police and FBI agents had been fairly certain that Cunanan was dead throughout the so-called siege. Using a heat-seeking camera in a helicopter circling overhead they had already confirmed precisely where Cunanan was located.

But as one FBI source later explained: "We couldn't be sure Cunanan wasn't just lying in a corner waiting for us, but we were pretty certain he was dead. The heat-seeking camera actually provided us with the image of his body as it lay there."

At ten P.M., FBI Special Agent Paul Phillips showed up in a dinner suit and bow tie as police and TV news helicopters continued whirling overhead. But the assembled media still had no information on whether a body had been found.

Then Miami Beach mayor Seymour Gelber told reporters waiting by the houseboat that he believed Cunanan had been found dead inside.

Rumors rapidly started circulating among the waiting reporters that there was a body inside the houseboat and it was Andrew Cunanan.

At 11:15 police finally confirmed that there was a corpse and that it resembled Cunanan.

Later that evening they even apologized for pretending they hadn't found the body during their first two searches of the vessel.

Miami Beach police chief Richard Barreto later blamed the misinformation on unspecified "logistical" problems.

But the FBI had a worrying logistical problem—Cunanan's face was so badly disfigured that it was impossible to tell if that was his corpse.

On the street, people expressed relief, but many expressed skepticism over the official version. Some speculated whether police may have shot Cunanan, but those present insisted they heard no shots other than the dull thud of tear gas grenades going off.

As 5:30 A.M., as the sun rose over the pastel shades of Miami's Art Deco skyline, Andrew Cunanan's body was finally removed from the houseboat on a gurney under a blue blanket. It was taken by hearse to Dade County Medical Center.

By six, following thumbprint checks, the FBI finally confirmed what the world had already presumed—it was the corpse of Andrew Cunanan.

At 6:30, the FBI updated their website entry on the Internet. On Cunanan's wanted poster two new words appeared—FOUND DEAD.

Cunanan left no suicide note to explain why he'd slaughtered at least five people in that gruesome trail of bloodshed across America.

Miami Beach police chief Richard Barreto told waiting reporters: "All across the nation our citizens can breathe a sigh of relief. The reign of terror brought on upon us by Andrew Cunanan is over."

And answering criticism of the combined police and FBI efforts to apprehend Cunanan, Chief Barreto said: "He made it forty blocks from the original scene. There was terrific pressure on him from law enforcement, media exposure and public vigilance. I think he was a desperate person; it was very difficult for him to move about."

FBI agent Paul Philip was even more upbeat although it appeared that pure luck played the biggest part in ending the manhunt.

"Listen, he managed to get forty blocks from the crime scene. That's the best he could do all this time. I think we did a pretty good job."

FBI spokeswoman Colleen Crowley said: "We were probably prepared for something like this. A person who is using desperate means and exhibiting this kind of violent behavior, you have to be prepared for a very violent conclusion."

Back on the houseboat on Indian Creek, investigators found Jeff Trail's Remington Peters pistol.

They refused to reveal if they'd found any other of Cunanan's possessions, but they were particularly interested in a small portable safe found close to Cunanan's body.

For a few hours after Cunanan's death various wild stories flew around among the assembled press corps. This included one that houseboat owner Torsten Reineck was a gay acquaintance of Andrew Cunanan.

Reineck, a flamboyant character, also owned the Apollo Spa and Health Club in Las Vegas, a small gay enclave. And German police revealed that Reineck was wanted on a Europe-wide arrest warrant for tax fraud involving $100,000.

But when investigators tracked the German down to his home in Las Vegas it turned out he was living happily with a woman and detectives were soon convinced he had no involvement with Cunanan other than being unlucky enough to have an empty houseboat that Cunanan had chosen as a secret refuge.

Next came the autopsy, and the pursuit of unanswered questions about the motives behind Andrew Cunanan's killing spree.

Principal among these were the tests to confirm Cunanan had AIDS, although under Florida state law it is unlikely if the results can ever be made public.

There was also a close examination of Cunanan's brain but, as one Miami coroner pointed out: "There wasn't that much left to look at."

Meanwhile caretaker Fernando Carreira told authorities he expected to be paid the $65,000 reward money offered for the capture of Andrew Cunanan. Their initial reaction was to refuse his claim.

Then Carreira filed a lawsuit against Miami Beach and Dade County to claim the reward: He was massively supported by local TV and radio, as well as in a petition that billed him as a hero.

Also in Miami Beach, it was claimed by the *Miami Herald* that tests on Cunanan's body showed he was *not* HIV-positive. At the time of writing this had still not been officially confirmed by the FBI or police.

The reaction to Cunanan's death in Miami was euphoric.

"It think it's great. Life can get back to some semblance of normality here," medical student Patric Chemaly told one reporter. "I think people were afraid to go out. They were always wondering if the trick they took home was Andrew."

The Versace family released a statement from the company headquarters in Milan: "The family offers its gratitude and sorrowful thanks to those who contributed to resolving the terrible killing of Gianni."

But it was Stanley Trail—father of victim number one, Jeff—who summed up the situation: "I'm very glad that he's been stopped and that nobody else got hurt. But I take no joy in his death. That doesn't help me at all. That's one of the bad things about him dying like this: Nobody will be able to ask him. Nobody will be able to tell me why this happened.''

By the weekend following Cunanan's death, FBI and police had started playing down the euphoria and were insisting that their job was not yet finished.

"This is far from over," one Miami Beach police spokesman told a British reporter. "Do you think somebody dies and we close the book and just walk away?"

Twenty-four

NO TURNING BACK

Ten .40 caliber bullets originally went missing from the box of Golden Saber cartridges left in Andrew Cunanan's nylon gym bag near Jeffrey Trail's bludgeoned body.

Three of these were subsequently expended in the killing of David Madson.

Another killed Bill Reese.

Two more ended the life of Gianni Versace.

And it took just one to end the biggest manhunt in American history . . .

Epilogue

The most important question in everyone's mind must now be why did Andrew Cunanan kill at least five people and then turn the gun on himself?

Cunanan had, in a matter of a few months, catapulted into the history books by developing a unique niche as a serial killer.

This was a criminal of our times. His "work," as criminologists call it, combined the culture of celebrity with the culture of murder. When it came to serial killers he had already broken all the rules.

By their very nature, serial killers are supposed to be given to feelings of invincibility. But no one has ever come across a phenomenon quite like Andrew Cunanan.

"The brazenness, the openness was highly unusual," said Ron Akers, an expert on serial killers and director of the Center of Criminality and Law at the University of Florida. "There was a lot of arrogance at work here. He was thumbing a nose at everyone."

These type of killers usually work in secret or seclusion or under cover of darkness. Not Andrew Cunanan. He killed Gianni Versace on Ocean Drive at breakfast time on a sunny Tuesday morning. It was a location filled with rollerbladers, the fabulous, the chic, and the sundrenched.

In the history of American murder, it's difficult to think of a venue as purposefully public, as theatrical, as the pink steps of Versace's palazzo.

But most significant of all: never has an American serial killer murdered someone as famous as Gianni Versace.

"Now he's famous too," said Jack Levin, professor of criminology at Northeastern University in Boston and an author of three books on serial killers and mass murderers. "As a rule, serial killers don't go after celebrities. Most serial killers target prostitutes and street people and old women living alone or small children—safe, conventional targets. Most serial killers would never use a firearm."

Four of Cunanan's victims died of bullet wounds, including himself.

"There isn't much that Cunanan shared with most serial killers," said Levin. "To begin with, most serial killers haven't been identified by police. But this guy left photographs, physical evidence, identification."

Dr. Helen Morrison, one of America's leading forensic phychiatrists who worked with the FBI on Gacy and Dahmer, said: "We are faced with a brand new type of murderer and that is one reason why there are so many unanswered questions. There is no comparison between Cunanan and any model we have. He is not a serial killer, not a spree killer, and certainly not a mass killer."

By way of heresy in law enforcement thinking, she added: "If someone doesn't fit, then maybe we should start getting rid of the boxes."

Was Cunanan insane? That, at least, would account for something. "The indications are that he was not insane," added Morrison.

Investigators have no doubt that Cunanan deliberately left his "calling cards" from the moment he began his killing spree in May, 1997.

In suburban Minneapolis he left a gym bag with his name

on it at the home of David Madson. Also found were an empty holster and a partially filled box of his signature ammunition: .40 caliber Golden Saber bullets.

When police found the red Chevy pickup Cunanan stole from his fourth victim, Bill Reese, they found a single blank check from the Bank of America with Cunanan's name clearly printed on it.

This wasn't the work of a careless man. This was a deliberate attempt to goad the investigators. Cunanan was telling them: "Come and get me if you can."

But the biggest problem facing the FBI and police in the hunt for Cunanan was how much publicity to give the case.

There were genuine fears that the intense international media coverage might fuel Cunanan's ego and encourage him to seek out new victims just to satisfy his lust for publicity.

"It was a real dilemma because we needed to publicize the case to increase the chance of him being spotted, but we also didn't want to encourage him to kill again," said one FBI agent.

Other homicide experts believe that Cunanan had actually long since convinced himself that he was superior to the authorities.

"He thought he was immune or impervious to capture," said Eric Hickey, a professor of criminology at California State University in Fresno. "Most serial killers are much more discrete, careful to hide the bodies. He was kind of like the Unabomber, who kept sending out more letters. Obviously, the more information you give out about yourself, the more likely you'll get caught."

Whether Cunanan should be classified as a spree killer or a serial killer has been a much-debated topic since Versace's murder.

Ronald Holmes, a University of Louisville criminologist and author of a book on serial killers, explained: "A spree killer is three or more murders in a thirty-day period. And

. when he went past that he became a full-blown serial killer.''

Spree killings involve multiple victims in many places in a short time, while serial killings involve multiple victims in separate incidents spread over time.

Experts like Ronald Holmes believe that a killer's motives can change in the middle of his spree of deaths.

''It doesn't have to make sense to you. It just has to make sense to him,'' said Holmes.

He is convinced there are other victims of Cunanan that police have not yet been made aware of. Notorious serial killer Ted Bundy once told Holmes that he hid some bodies but not others, leaving them as ''an advertisement'' to let people know he was still around.

''The killing of Versace was to him a major coup or accomplishment,'' explained Vernon Geberth, author of *Practical Homicide Investigation*, a textbook for homicide detectives.

''He got to kill someone of international fame and he also got to shove it up the nose of the FBI and all the police who were looking for him.

''If you take a look at the dynamics of the killing of this designer, he was basically killing the person that he could never be . . . A lot of folks who do this feel a sense of superiority over the police. The police were basically impotent to him. By doing this, he not only got to validate his own superiority, he got to make a statement.''

The FBI has refused to speculate on whether Cunanan has killed others. But many disagree.

Perhaps the most baffling aspect of the case was that Cunanan did not even fit the stereotypical picture of a serial killer as a brooding loner, full of hostility for the world.

''So what spurred this murderous campaign?'' asked San Francisco State University criminologist Michael Rustigan. ''If he did get AIDS then he could quickly have developed a grudge against the wealthy gay men he consorted with.''

Former FBI agent Richard Ressler, who profiled serial killers for fifteen years, has closely watched the Cunanan case unfold.

"He had relationships with several young men and one left him," said Ressler. "He was having financial problems. All of these dynamics were pulling on this guy. Being self-centered and narcissistic, these had a special stress. And I suspect this guy probably had contracted AIDS."

Authorities always said he would either kill himself or someone else eventually—and they were proved fatally correct.

Cunanan's ability to change his appearance also hampered his hunters, but there was little doubt he also had a great deal of luck.

The fingerprints were blurred at best and even the videotape of Cunanan running away showed nothing more than a fuzzy image of a man.

Cunanan was also extremely careful not to use his credit cards in case police used the records to track him.

"The more he got away with, the more dangerous he became. He wouldn't have hesitated to murder again if someone got in his way," added ex-FBI agent William Tafoya.

But other experts, like Dr. Reid Morley, a psychologist and author of *The Psychopathic Mind* believe that Cunanan wanted to be caught. "We had him actively leaving evidence to link him very quickly and very directly to Versace. We had him saying: 'I did this, and also did the one just before.' It looked very purposeful. And the more frightening aspect was that he seemed to be becoming more organized."

And two prominent psychiatrists summed up Cunanan's cross-country killings.

"He was in complete control," said one Chicago expert.

New York psychiatrist Paul Salkin added: "He was a complete chameleon. He seemed to adjust his persona to his surroundings. We were talking about a multiple personality here. He certainly had multiple appearances.''

Bill Hagmaier, the chief of the FBI's Child Abduction and Serial Killer Unit, reckoned that Cunanan had begun as a spree killer—murdering his first victims in a rush, motivated by rage or vendetta.

But then he evolved into a classic serial killer. ''After the first few times,'' said Hagmaier, ''the killing got easier. The killer began to feel absolute power over human beings.''

In other words serial murderers become intoxicated by their celebrity and have to kill again to maintain the ''euphoria of murder.'' Like addicts, they eventually become strung out—and make a mistake.

Cataloging all the different ways Cunanan is alleged to have killed—friends and strangers, with guns, tools, quickly and slowly—Thomas Epach, the chief of criminal prosecutions for Cook County, Illinois, said:''It was like watching a weather map. This killer was the consummate criminal storm.''

All across the country, there are lots of other storm watchers sleeping easy in their beds for the first time in months.

Andrew Cunanan's life was a psychodrama played for maximum applause—or horror. It was one long divide between reality and fantasy, a widening and now fatal chasm.

TEN MOST WANTED FUGITIVE

WANTED BY THE FBI

Toll Free Hot Line – 1-888-FBI-9800

ARMED AND EXTREMELY DANGEROUS

Andrew Phillip Cunanan

THE CRIME

Andrew Phillip Cunanan has been charged with the murder of David Madson in Chisago County, Minnesota, and unlawful flight to avoid prosecution in this case. He has been charged with the murder of Lee Miglin in Chicago, Illinois and with Crime on a Government Reservation-Murder for the murder of William Reese, in Pennsville, New Jersey. Authorities believe that he fled Minnesota in Madson's Jeep Cherokee.

Andrew Phillip Cunanan

FOUND DEAD

DOB:	August 31, 1969
Sex:	Male
Height:	5' 10"
Weight:	160-180 pounds
Hair:	Dark Brown
Eyes:	Brown
Race:	White
Alias:	Andrew Phillip DeSilva
	Drew Cunningham

Several days later, authorities discovered the Jeep abandoned, on a street where Chicago, Illinois authorities were investigating a murder. Discovered missing from this crime scene was the victim's 1994 Lexus, which later turned up in a cemetery parking lot in Pennsville, New Jersey.

In Pennsville, New Jersey, authorities were called to a cemetery when the caretaker failed to return home from work on Friday, 5/9/97. The caretaker was discovered murdered. His vehicle was also reported to be missing.

The caretaker's vehicle, described as a red 1995 Chevy pick-up, was recovered in Miami Beach, Florida, on July 17, 1997, near the scene of the murder of Gianni Versace. Cunanan is being sought for questioning in connection with the murder of Versace.

REMARKS

Cunanan may wear prescription eyeglasses. He allegedly has ties to the gay community. Cunanan has been known to significantly change his appearance.

REWARD: The FBI is offering $10,000 for information leading to the apprehension of Cunanan.

If you have any information concerning this case take no action yourself. Contact the local police department or the nearest **FBI Office.**

Gianni Versace had a clear vision of how he would like to die in a perfect world.

On the eve of his fiftieth birthday in December, 1996, he told an Italian newspaper he imagined himself dying by a tranquil lakeside, like the scion of a declining aristocratic family. His epitaph, he hoped, would say he was a man who took pleasure in breaking conventions and mixing genres, eras, and social classes.

But it was not to be . . .